Business Lobbies and the Power Structure in America

Business Lobbies and the Power Structure in America

Evidence and Arguments

David C. D. Jacobs

Q

QUORUM BOOKS
Westport, Connecticut • London

Library of Congress Cataloging-in-Publication Data

Jacobs, David C., 1953–
    Business lobbies and the power structure in America : evidence and
arguments / David C. D. Jacobs.
        p.   cm.
    Includes bibliographical references and index.
    ISBN 1–56720–041–9 (alk. paper)
    1. Business and politics—United States.   I. Title.
JK467.J33   1999
322′.3′0973—dc21   98–27836

British Library Cataloguing in Publication Data is available.

Library of Congress Catalog Card Number: 98–27836
ISBN: 1–56720–041–9

First published in 1999

Quorum Books, 88 Post Road West, Westport, CT 06881
An imprint of Greenwood Publishing Group, Inc.

Printed in the United States of America

The paper used in this book complies with the
Permanent Paper Standard issued by the National
Information Standards Organization (Z39.48–1984).

10 9 8 7 6 5 4 3 2

Copyright Acknowledgments

The author and publisher gratefully acknowledge permission for use of the following material:

Excerpts from *BSR Mission Statement*. 1997. From Business for Social Responsibility. Http://www.bsr.org.

Excerpts from review of Max Green's "Epitaph of American Labor" by David Jacobs. Published in *ILR Review*. October 1997. Ithaca, NY.

Excerpts of "Employment Policy Principles" from *Keeping America Competitive: Employment Policy for the Twenty-first Century* by Edward E. Potter and Judith A. Youngman. 1995. Lakewood, CO: Glenbridge Publishing.

Excerpts from "Labor and Social Legislation in the United States: Business Obstructionism and Accommodation" by David Jacobs. Published in *Labor Studies Journal*, Vol. 23, No. 2, Summer 1998.

Excerpts from author interview with Professor Nancy Bagranoff, American University. Washington, D.C. August 15, 1997. Printed with the permission of Nancy Bagranoff.

Excerpts from author interview with Professor Kathleen Getz. Washington, D.C. September 15, 1997. Printed with the permission of Kathleen Getz.

Excerpts from author interview with Susan Spriggs. Washington, D.C. August 15, 1997. Printed with the permission of Susan Spriggs.

Excerpts from author interview with Leon Shull. Washington, D.C. August 25, 1997. Printed with the permission of Leon Shull.

To the Nemeth-Benhaim-Dulk-Jacobs families:
to Jacob, Magda, Colette, Milton, George, Renée, and Valerie.
Love and thanks.

My appreciation to Brenna Isman and Allison Anderson for research assistance.

Contents

Introduction

In his *Dispute Resolution*, John Dunlop (1984) deplored the resistance of most U.S. business associations to dialog with organized labor concerning public policy initiatives. He asked, "How is one to account for [management's] intransigence at the confederation level?" (Dunlop 1984, p. 124).

Dunlop completed his work as chair of the Clinton administration's Commission on the Future of Worker/Management Relations in 1994. In this forum as in so many others, he sought to encourage labor and management to seek consensus and make policy together. There has been little evidence that any grand labor-management bargain that would facilitate union organizing as well as provide some form of relief to employers was at all likely.

Sanford Jacoby (1991) submits that American employers are exceptional in their anti-unionism and anti-statism, more resistant to compromise than European business. He suggests that European business has been motivated to compromise with government, labor, and other organized constituencies because of the greater threat of the radical left on the Continent.[1] In his *Business Lobbies: the Public Good and the Bottom Line*, Sar Levitan (Levitan and Cooper 1984, p. 28) noted, "The business community has, for the most part, opposed social welfare and labor programs as they have been proposed in Congress; at least initially, all they can see is the cost involved."

On the other hand, many college texts in business and society imply that corporate responsiveness to stakeholders is on the advance. Scholars debate various notions of stakeholder management. Companies routinely cite their social responsibility in their appeals to consumers. In a popular text, *Business and Society: Corporate Strategy, Public Policy, Ethics*, James E. Post and his co-authors (1996, p. 20) write:

What is emerging in the view of some observers . . . is a new "social contract" between the corporation, its employees, and other stakeholders. . . . The new social contract implies that stakeholders can reasonably expect that managers will acknowledge those relationships, deal with the impacts of their decisions, and respond to the people that are touched by the corporation's activities.

What is the underlying reality? Are U.S. firms increasingly willing to pursue dialog with workers and other social groups in an effort to shape a new social contract, or are they hostile to such compromise?

I have reviewed documentary and secondary sources that reveal the activities and programs of business confederations such as the Chamber of Commerce, National Association of Manufacturers (NAM), and Business Roundtable. I find that most business associations subscribe to a philosophy that rejects the notion of compromise with stakeholders, particularly organized labor, in the formulation of private practice or public policy. On the other hand, individual businesses seek to accommodate stakeholders to varying degrees. Dissenting voices in the business community challenging the hard-line approach of the business associations are weak and seldom effective. The Republican party frequently intervenes in the affairs of business confederations to strengthen their resolve against compromise. In doing so, they are doing the will of many leading corporations.

In the following chapters I will provide portraits of business associations and case studies of business association activism on health care reform, occupational disease notification, civil rights, and other issues. Each case provides evidence of business associations' hostility to compromise on labor and social legislation (with one exception that still lends credence to the overall argument). (See Figure 1.)

In addition to the case studies, this book features primary documents outlining disparate business views on social security, social responsibility, and international competitiveness. I have included interviews with a reform-oriented businesswoman, a business academic, and a liberal lobbyist. I consider the roles of state politics, international competition, think tanks, and political language in sustaining the rigid stance of mainstream business lobbies. These elements should further clarify my analysis of the divisions within the business community.

This essay owes some of its tone to Robert Brady's *Business as a System of Power*, an influential work of political sociology published in 1943. Brady argued that powerful business interests responded to challenges from labor and other social movements in one of two ways: acceptance of their diminished authority and pursuit of compromise, or withdrawal of support for democratic institutions. He considered the case of Nazi Germany and noted the degree to which American business was willing to cooperate with the Nazis, as well as inconclusive evidence that some American executives contemplated revolution against the New Deal.

Figure 1
Summary Table of Legislative Initiatives, Supporters, and Opponents

Mandated Health Insurance

Supporters: National Leadership Coalition for Health Care Reform; Health Care Reform Project; American Airlines; Chrysler; Southern California Edison; etc.

Mandated Health Insurance

Opponents: National Federation of Independent Business; Chamber of Commerce (withdrew initial support); National Association of Manufacturers; Business Roundtable; etc.

Occupational Disease Notification

Supporters: Chemical Manufacturers Association; Manville Corporation; American Cyanamid; etc.

Occupational Disease Notification

Opponents: Labor Policy Association; Chamber of Commerce; National Hotel and Motel Association; National Federation of Independent Business; etc.

Family Medical Leave Act

Supporters: Business for Social Responsibility; Lotus; Stride-Rite; Reebok; Timberland; Quad Graphics; Body Shop; etc.

Family Medical Leave Act

Opponents: Chamber of Commerce; Labor Policy Association; National Federation of Independent Business; etc.

Civil Rights Act of 1991

Supporters: Business Roundtable; AT&T; etc.

Civil Rights Act of 1991

Opponents: Chamber of Commerce; National Federation of Independent Business; etc.

He explained:

Businessmen all over the world are engaged in weaving parallel webs of control. . . . a point is reached at which, willy-nilly, a choice of direction is forced upon the businessman. One way leads to the shaking off of all popular restraints on such cumulative powers and to shaping the contours and determining the content of economic policies pregnant with far-reaching political, social, and cultural implications. This is the totalitarian road. . . .

The contrasting choice is to force the growth of a sense of responsibility to democratic institutions, not by transmuting arbitrary controls into series of patriarchal relationships . . . but by steadily widening the latitude for direct public participation in the formulation of economic policies affecting the public interests. (Brady, p. 2)

Brady and muckraking journalist George Seldes (1950) both viewed the National Association of Manufacturers and the Chamber of Commerce as authoritarian, if not fascistic, in their politics. Brady and Seldes wrote decades ago, and their arguments may have little validity now. However, they were right to explore the influence of business associations on the character of business and politics in the United States. Institutions of this kind shape as well as reflect the development of their constituencies. The NAM, Chamber, and Business Roundtable may, in fact, have elements of a "system of power."

One of my assumptions in this analysis is that public policymaking is enhanced and justice served when social groups participate in dialog. John Stuart Mill's *On Liberty*, John Dewey's concept of social intelligence, and Michael Piore's critique of neoclassical economics reinforce these assumptions. First, Mill argued that free debate, the interplay of disparate views, was conducive to the discovery of truth, regardless of the merit of one's own position. "If all of mankind minus one, were of one opinion, and only one person were of the contrary opinion, mankind would be no more justified in silencing that one person, than he, if he had the power, would be justified in silencing mankind" (Mill 1947, p. 16). Second, John Dewey believed that knowledge is inherently social, that the insights of the group are richer when combined than is the contribution of any one member. In fact, knowledge does not exist unless it is susceptible to communication to and review by others. It cannot exist in solopsistic isolation in the mind of one individual. Moreover, Dewey insisted on the importance of input from the weakest members of society, without which the full impact of institutional decisions cannot be known.

Dewey wrote:

While what we call intelligence may be distributed in unequal amounts, it is the democratic faith that it is sufficiently general so that each individual has something to contribute, and the value of each contribution can be assessed only as it enters into the final pooled intelligence constituted by the contributions of all. Every authoritarian scheme, on the contrary, assumes that its value may be assessed by some *prior* principle, if not of family and birth or race and color or possession of material wealth, then by the position and rank a person occupies in the existing social scheme.

Third, Michael Piore (1995) explains that communications depend upon an iterative and interactive (hermeneutic) process in which sender and receiver exchange cues clarifying meaning. In a sense, meaning is negotiated. Piore argues that the social character of knowledge and the hermeneutic dimension of communications belie the notions of market exchange and rational individualism that are central to market economics. The market transaction in the neoclassical model is a poor approximation of human behavior. Human interaction is a multilateral *process*, not a succession of bilateral deals.

The market model arguably constitutes an authoritarian scheme (of the sort Dewey had in mind) in that it implicitly attributes just authority to positions and ranks in organizations if they have been determined in free markets. The leaders of business lobbies argue that their private behavior as business leaders has been tested by the market and that engagement in dialog with other organized groups is likely to blunt market forces to the detriment of all. House Majority Leader Richard Armey derisively calls those businesses open to dialog "prags."

The works of Mill, Dewey, and Piore provide the philosophical support for my assumption that dialog among social groups is superior to reliance upon market forces for social provisions.

Cohen and Rogers (1992) argue that groups can improve the quality of information for policymakers and citizens as they illuminate political debate. Organized groups may improve the position of the weak; organizing pools the resources of the weak and provides countervailing power. Cohen and Rogers submit that "groups improve an imperfect system of interest representation by making it more fine-grained, attentive to preference intensities, and representative of diverse views." Groups are sometimes an alternative to markets and public hierarchies.

There is always the danger that organized interests may conclude agreements that harm the unorganized or that the leaders of these interests may disregard the concerns of those whom they represent. The critics of "interest group liberalism" and "corporatism" (for example, political scientist Theodore Lowi [1969]) have argued that an undemocratic, bureaucratic conservatism unavoidably results. (Lowi predicted the "atrophy of institutions of popular control" and "the maintenance of old and the creation of new structures of privilege.") Certainly not all compromises are good. Some are inherently corrupt. However, I believe that the business lobbies' resistance to bargains (even when this stance is consistent with free market doctrine) poses the greater danger of poor policymaking and injustice.

The reader may protest that my critique of the business lobbies is harsh. If one accepts the market paradigm at face value, one would regard business lobbies' defense of the free market to be in the interest of all. In this light, the business lobbies' opposition to social legislation satisfies their public responsibilities, and any concessions to the advocates of social legislation would harm the very individuals seeking protection. The free market conservative is likely to praise employers who consistently oppose the agenda of organized labor and other stakeholder groups. This perspective will be reflected in some of the documents and dialogs in the chapters to follow. Even if the reader agrees with the business lobbies' approach to social legislation, I hope that he or she will find my characterization of the divisions within the business community to be instructive and persuasive.

NOTE

1. Jacoby cites works by Gert Hofstede and Reinhard Bendix suggesting that American managers are more individualistic than managers elsewhere in the world. They are somewhat less inclined than European managers to surrender authority to employers' associations for the purpose of negotiating binding agreements with government (or labor). Jacoby argues that American industrialization occurred with a minimum of government involvement, contributing to employers' limited sense of the legitimacy of government action and the benefits of social legislation (Jacoby 1991).

REFERENCES

Brady, R. (1943). *Business as a system of power*. New York: Columbia University Press.

Cohen, J., and J. Rogers. (1992). "Secondary associations and democratic governance." *Politics and Society* 20:393–472.

Dewey, J. (1939). "Democracy and educational administration." In J. Ratner, ed., *Intelligence in the modern world*. New York: Random House, pp. 400–404.

Dunlop, J. (1984). *Dispute resolution: Negotiations and consensus building*. Dover, Mass.: Auburn House.

Jacoby, S., ed. (1991). *Masters to managers: Historical and comparative perspectives on American employers*. New York: Columbia University Press.

Levitan, S. A., and M. Cooper. (1984). *Business lobbies: The public good and the bottom line*. Baltimore: Johns Hopkins University.

Lowi, T. J. (1969). *The end of liberalism*. New York: Norton.

Mill, J. S. (1947). *On liberty*. New York: Appleton-Century-Crofts.

Piore, M. (1995). *Beyond liberalism*. Cambridge, Mass.: Harvard University Press.

Post, J. E., W. C. Frederick, A. T. Lawrence, and J. Weber. (1996). *Business and society: Corporate strategy, public policy, ethics*. New York: McGraw-Hill.

Seldes, G. (1950). "Leaders of native fascism form committee of 12 to recruit army of reaction, foist views on US." *In Fact* (July 3): p. 1.

CHAPTER ONE ————————————————————

Sophisticated Conservatives

There are significant ideological divisions within the business community. Despite the anti-unionism of the vast majority of businesses, some are open to dialog with organized labor. "Sophisticated conservatives" (Mills 1948, pp. 25–27), corporate leaders seeking an accommodation with organized labor and the welfare state, were prominent within the business community of the 1940s. Sociologist C. Wright Mills (1948, pp. 23–27) argued that conservatism comes in at least two forms: "sophisticated" and "practical." The sophisticated conservatives are corporate executives who are prepared to make small concessions to unions and to accept increased government regulation of the economy so as to preserve their power. They "hold that unions are a stabilizing force and should be encouraged as a counter-force against radical movements." Sophisticated conservatives "would have the trade union leader end up in their personnel and public relations departments, as a junior lieutenant of the captains of industry. " Practical conservatives are business leaders who tolerate no compromise with organized labor on the shopfloor or in Congress. They "represent pure and simple anti-unionism, fighting labor because they know how very practical most of labor's activities are." Practical conservatives are likely to share a fundamental opposition to good faith bargaining with lower status groups in any forum, given that such bargains tend to violate individualistic, free market principles.

Peter Viereck, a professor of history at Mount Holyoke, was an articulate proponent of sophisticated conservatism. In his *Conservatism Revisited*, he asserted, "Since the industrial revolution, conservatism is neither justifiable nor effective unless it has roots in the factories and trade unions" (Viereck 1949, p. 12). He ultimately found the conservative movements of the 1950s and 1960s to be largely lacking in sympathy for the working class and uncritical in their embrace of laissez-faire.

Sophisticated conservatives have played a critical role in the work of the National Civic Federation in the early 1900s, in the projects of the National Planning Association in the postwar era, and in the activities of the Committee for Economic Development. All three of these groups have provided for the representation of non-business constituencies (labor, the professions, academics and university administrators, etc.) for the purpose of dialog. On the other hand, the Chamber of Commerce, National Association of Manufacturers, Business Roundtable, Labor Policy Association, and other mainstream business confederations have been dominated by practical conservatives and have sought to undermine the prospects for labor-management compromise in policymaking. Moreover, the organizations open to compromise have met considerable opposition from mainstream business associations and have seldom sustained their moderate posture.

For example, in the early 1970s, the Committee for Economic Development (CED), a panel of top executives, academics, and university presidents, embraced an expansive model of corporate social responsibility. The CED report *Social Responsibilities of Business Corporations* noted: "The modern professional manager also regards himself, not as an owner disposing of personal property as he sees fit, but as a trustee balancing the interests of many diverse participants and constituents in the enterprise" (1971, p. 22).

Scholar Rensis Likert contributed an essay to another CED report, *A New Rationale for Corporate Social Policy*, in which he argued that many firms routinely liquidate valuable human resource assets to boost apparent earnings (Baumol et al. 1970). W.C. Frederick (1981, pp. 20–28) argues that the political mood of the late 1960s and early 1970s—the emergence of environmental, consumer, and civil rights movements—compelled employers to consider new responsibilities. By 1979, conservative critics had persuaded the CED to abandon its conciliatory posture. The organization published "Redefining Government's Role in the Market System," which reflected the suspicion of most conservatives with respect to government initiatives (Frederick 1981, pp. 20–28).

In the 1980s and 1990s, evidence of sophisticated conservatism within business associations has diminished. Business lobbies oppose social legislation with near unanimity. When the Family and Medical Leave Act passed in 1993, it was with the near universal opposition of organized business. The Chamber of Commerce, the National Federation of Independent Business (NFIB), the Society for Human Resource Management (SHRM), and other groups were opponents of the measure, which merely guaranteed twelve weeks of unpaid leave to employees of most companies. Diane DuVal's testimony on behalf of Lotus and a dissident group, Business for Social Responsibility (BSR), represented the only favorable testimony on the Family and Medical Leave Act from the business community. The initiative passed because of the support of the Clinton administration and many in Congress who were prepared to ignore the counsel of business in this one instance (*In Business* 1993).

Business for Social Responsibility was founded in part to counter the influence of the Chamber of Commerce and other conservative business groups. However, BSR has recently sought to be inclusive at the expense of political coherence. It now avoids questions of public policy. I will explore the sources of instability in alternative business organizations in a subsequent chapter.

REFERENCES

Baumol, W., R. Likert, H. C. Wallich, and J. J. McGowan. (1970). *A new rationale for corporate social policy*. New York: Committee for Economic Development.

Committee for Economic Development. (1971). *Social responsibilities of business corporations*. New York: Committee for Economic Development.

Frederick, W. C. (1981). "Free market vs. social responsibility." *California Management Review* 23: 20–28.

In Business. (1993). "Spotlighting social responsibility." *In Business* (November/December): 34.

Mills, C. W. (1948). *The new men of power: America's labor leaders*. New York: Harcourt Brace.

Viereck, P. (1949). *Conservatism revisited: The revolt against revolt: 1815–1949*. New York: Charles Scribner's Sons.

CHAPTER TWO

Mainstream Business Lobbies

Many business confederations have been hostile to labor since their founding days. The Business Roundtable (BR) was formed by the merger of two groups sharing an uncompromising approach to labor issues—the Construction Users Anti-Inflation Roundtable and the Labor Law Study Group—and a third organization, the March Group. Member businesses (all from the Fortune 500 and including almost all of the Fortune 100) were particularly concerned by the power of labor in construction and sought to advance a non-union sector in the construction industry to reduce the cost of new facilities. They had formed the "Nothing Committee" to quietly organize a propaganda offensive (including efforts to co-opt leading liberal intellectuals and influence television programming) against the liberal NLRB of the Kennedy and Johnson administrations (Gross 1995, pp. 192–216).

The Roundtable appeared to mellow in the mid-1970s, and BR members participated in the deliberations of the Labor-Management Group chaired by economist John

Dunlop. The *Daily Labor Report* (1975, p. C-1) noted a "revamped business stance toward Washington . . . on labor issues." Alcoa's chief executive officer John C. Harper, a BR member, said that the tendency of major business executives to assume an antagonistic posture toward labor and big-city Democrats had been modified. However, the Roundtable still resisted any compromise on labor law reform (strongly advocated by trade unionists who noted the decreasing effectiveness of the National Labor Relations Board). The Roundtable overrode the objections of some members (Reginald Jones of General Electric, Irving Shapiro of DuPont, and Thomas Murphy of General Motors [Daily Labor Report 1978, p. C-1]) who argued for neutrality and joined a business phalanx of opposition to reform in the interests of workers. Labor leaders were surprised at the level of opposition the proposed reform received since their focus was repeated labor law violators like J. P. Stevens rather than mainstream big business (Levitan and Cooper 1984; Dunlop 1984). The strongly anti-union Labor Policy Association has ordinarily functioned as the labor relations arm of the BR and will be described in considerable detail in the next chapter.

The Business Roundtable is often described as a sophisticated, socially concerned force within the business community, committed to rational discourse with public policy makers, rather than to the pursuit of free markets at all costs. The moderate reputation of the Roundtable is belied by its behavior in critical situations. The Roundtable tends in the final analysis not to stray too far from the narrow concerns of the executives most at risk or from an anti-labor trajectory.

The National Association of Manufacturers (NAM) was founded by open-shop employers in 1894, and this anti-union theme has been sustained over the years, most recently by NAM's affiliate, the Council for Positive Employee Relations.[1] While the Association was established ostensibly to promote foreign trade, a major coal strike early in its existence brought latent interests in industrial relations issues to the fore. The NAM provided many employers with a forum for anti-New Deal activities in the 1930s. Like other business lobbies, the NAM shows little evidence of having accepted either collective bargaining or the welfare state today. While many large, unionized firms belong to the NAM, conservative members have obstructed any conciliatory gestures toward the Clinton administration on health care reform (Levitan and Cooper 1984). The NAM's conservatism is reinforced by the especially right-wing affiliates from southern states; these branches often work closely with member companies on anti-union drives. About 13,500 firms currently belong to the organization.

In a *Harvard Business Review* article, Alfred Cleveland noted the extreme conservatism of the NAM of the 1940s:

Without exception the measures favored by the NAM provided some sort of aid to business and industry. Without exception rigid opposition was maintained against similar assistance to other groups and against all regulatory measures pertaining to industry. . . . The branding of social security as totalitarian when it was first proposed, the wartime barrage of propaganda creating the impression that the government and labor were using the emergency as a means of furthering their own antidemocratic ends, and the ready willingness of the Association's policy makers to lay the blame for all social and economic ills at the feet of other groups or institutions offer further evidence of the narrow base from which the Association has operated. . . . The extreme conservatism of the NAM . . . is reason for real alarm. (1948, pp. 357–359)

There is little evidence that the NAM has significantly moderated its stance since the 1940s.

The Chamber of Commerce was founded with the help of the National Association of Manufacturers in 1912. President William Taft directed his Secretaries of Labor and Commerce to bring local commercial associations to Washington to organize a new national structure representing business. Despite the involvement of government, the Chamber soon found its mission in opposing government activism as well as organized labor. (In the early days of the Chamber and in the immediate postwar period, there was greater internal debate than now characterizes the organization.) In many states and local communities, Chamber affiliates have been the dominant political powers, particularly in the south. The generally doctrinaire laissez-faire ideology of the Chamber of Commerce is reinforced by its relationship to the Republican party (as it was in previous years by its relationship to conservative southern Democrats). About 215,000 businesses are currently members. There is sentiment within both the Chamber and NAM for a merger of the two organizations, but past efforts to do so have failed (Levitan and Cooper 1984).

The National Federation of Independent Business (founded in 1943) represents small business (the vast majority with ten or fewer employees) altogether opposed to legislative initiatives that would sustain enterprises as well as enhance collective goods. The NFIB has opposed increases in the minimum wage, medicare, safety and health legislation, and the like with complete consistency since its founding. The organization frequently polls its 607,000 members, many of whom are extremely conservative, and reaffirms its uncompromising course (Levitan and Cooper 1984, p. 41).

National Small Business United (NSBU) consists of businesses somewhat larger than those belonging to the National Federation of Independent Business and tends to favor a more conciliatory strategy toward the government. This is almost exclusively a matter of tactics, however. NSBU's leaders note that businesses who refuse to entertain dialog with regard to public policy find that injurious choices have been made in their absence (NSBU 1993).

NOTE

1. Formerly the Committee on a Union-Free Environment. Both names were intentionally ambiguous. It is unclear from the names whether the purpose of the committee is to assist existing non-union firms or to campaign for the abolition of unionism altogether. Labor protest resulted in the assignment of a new name for the organization, but the harsh and punitive tone of the document, "Staying Union-Free," published by the committee, belies any assertions of benevolent concern for employees.

REFERENCES

Cleveland, A. (1948). "NAM: Spokesman for industry?" *Harvard Business Review*: 26 (May): 353–371.

Daily Labor Report. (1975). "Revamped business stance toward Washington noted on labor issues." *Daily Labor Report* (February 10): C-1.

Daily Labor Report. (1978). "Angry labor members put the Labor-Management Group on ice despite some favorable notices." *Daily Labor Report* (August 30): C-1.

Dunlop, J. (1984). *Dispute resolution: Negotiations and consensus building*. Dover, Mass.: Auburn House.

Gross, J. (1995). *Subverting the promise*. Philadelphia: Temple University Press.

Levitan, S. A., and M. Cooper. (1984). *Business lobbies: The public good and the bottom line*. Baltimore: Johns Hopkins University Press.

NSBU. (1993). "President's health care plan draws mixed response from small business owners." Press release, September 21.

The Role of the Labor Policy Association

The Labor Policy Association (LPA) was founded in 1939 by corporate executives worried about the power of organized labor and the role of the National Labor Relations Board. The LPA supported efforts to amend the National Labor Relations Act to increase employers' and individuals' ability to oppose unionization and thus contributed to the enactment of the Taft-Hartley Act. Kenneth McGuiness, formerly Associate General Counsel of the NLRB, Special Counsel to the House Education and Labor Committee, and an architect of the Landrum-Griffin Act, assumed the position of Director of LPA in 1968. He was succeeded by Jeffrey C. McGuiness in 1988. R. Conrad Cooper, formerly an executive with United States Steel, provided guidance to the Association in the 1970s. More recently, assistance was provided by G. John Tysse, formerly Director of Labor Law for the Chamber of Commerce, and Daniel V. Yager, formerly Republican Labor Counsel to the House Education and Labor Committee. Throughout the history of the LPA, it has evidently worked closely with the Republican party, the Chamber, and leading corporations, always advancing an agenda of practical conservatism.

Senior human resource management officers from 230 major corporations support the LPA. (See Table 3.1 for a list of corporate members of LPA.) Unionized Xerox and General Motors are member organizations, as well as militantly anti-union McDonald's, PepsiCo, and Marriott. The LPA's Board of Directors includes the Vice Presidents for Human Resources at Chrysler, AT&T, Boeing, Ford, and the United Parcel Service, all unionized enterprises (Labor Policy Association 1993).

The McGuiness and Williams law firm with which the LPA is associated employs a group of practicing attorneys who combine legislative and litigation experience. In addition to the *amicus curiae* legal briefs prepared by staff attorneys on behalf of management, the firm also supports the work of the Equal Employment Advisory Council, which assists employers in responding to civil rights challenges.

The LPA's annual report states, "One valuable benefit provided by Association membership is its network of senior level corporate human resource executives from a broad cross-section of industry and the opportunity to build relationships that is not available through most industry trade associations" (Labor Policy Association 1993, p. 8). Apparently, even executives from Fortune 500 firms with well-established relationships with trade unions value the LPA despite its rigid conservatism. Perhaps corporations routinely contribute to a variety of organizations with widely varied perspectives in order to maintain cordial relations with all elements of the business community (thus attaining a measure of unity). Moreover, the LPA's enhanced power and influence in the context of a Republican Congress are such that more "liberal" (less anti-union) corporations may contribute for reasons of expediency. (In a conservative political environment, the benefits of affiliation with the LPA might be greater than those that attend participation

Table 3.1
Member Corporations of Labor Policy Association

3M	Bank of America
ALCOA	Baxter Healthcare
AMAX	Bechtel
APASCO	Bell Atlantic
ARA Services	BellSouth
AT&T	Bethlehem Steel
Abbott Laboratories	Beverly Enterprises
Air Products and Chemicals	Boeing
Alabama Power	Boise Cascade
Alexander and Alexander	Borden
Allied-Signal	Bridgestone/Firestone
American Airlines	Bristol Myers-Squibb
American Brands	Brown and Williamson Tobacco
American Cyanamid	Brunswick Bowling and Bill
American Express	Burlington Industries
American Standard	CBI Industries
Ameritech	CIGNA
Amoco	COMPAQ Computer
Anheuser-Busch	Campbell Soup
Armco	Carter Hawley Hale Stores
Armstrong World Industries	Caterpillar
Ashland Oil	Central States Can
Atlantic Richfield	Ceridian
BFGoodrich	Champion International
BP America	Chevron
Ball	Chrysler
Baltimore Gas and Electric	Ciba-Geigy

Cincinnati Bell Telephone

Citibank

Citizens Financial Group

Coca-Cola

Computer Associates Int'l.

Computer Sciences

Cooper Industries

Corning

Cox Enterprises

Cyprus Minerals

Deere

Depository Trust

Detroit Edison

Digital Equipment

Domino's Pizza

Donaldson

Dow Chemical

Duke Power

E.I. DuPont De Nemours

Eastman Kodak

Eaton

Emerson Electric

Equitable Life Assurance Society

Exxon

FMC

Federal Express

Federal Mogul

Federated Department Stores

Florida Power

Ford Motor

GTE

Gannett

GenCorp.

General Dynamics

General Electric

General Mills

General Motors

Georgia-Pacific

Goldman, Sachs & Co.

Goodyear Tire and Rubber

Greyhound Lines

Halliburton

Hallmark Cards

Harris

Harsco

Hershey Foods

Hewlett-Packard

Hilton Hotels

Hoescht Celanese

Honeywell

Hughes Aircraft

IBM

ITT

Illinois Tool Works

Ingersoll-Rand

Inland Steel

International Paper

Invacare

J.C. Penney

J.P. Morgan

Jefferson Smurfit

Johnson & Johnson

Kellogg

LTV

Leggett & Platt

Lockheed

MCI

Marriott

Marsh & McLennan

Martin Marietta

Maytag

McDonald's

McDonnell Douglas

Mead

Melville

Merck and Co.

Meredith Corp.

Merrill Lynch

Methodist Hospital System

Metropolitan Life Insurance

Mobil

Monsanto

Motorola

Murray Ohio Manufacturing

Mutual of Omaha

NYNEX

National Gypsum

Nestle USA

Newmont Gold

Norfolk Southern

Northern Telecom

Northrop

Occidental Petroleum

Olin

Oralco Management Services

PPG Industries

PACCAR

Pacific Gas and Electric

Pacific Telesis Group

Pennzoil

PepsiCo

Pfizer

Philadelphia Electric

Pillsbury

Premark International

Procter and Gamble

Promus Companies

Prudential Insurance

Public Service of Colorado

RJR Nabisco

R.R. Donnelly and Sons

Raytheon

Reliance Electric

Rochester Telephone

Rockwell International

Rubbermaid

Ryder System	Textron
Sara Lee	Thiokol
Sea-Land Service	Timken
Shearson Lehman Brothers	Travelers Insurance
Shell Oil	USG
Society Corp.	USWest
South Bay Growers	USX
Southern California Edison	Union Carbide
Southwestern Bell	Union Pacific
Sprint	Unisys
Sun Company	United Parcel Service
Sundstrand	United Technologies
Sunsweet Growers	Unocal
TRW	Vought Aircraft
Tandem Computers	Walgreen Company
Tenneco	Westinghouse Electric
Texaco	Weyerhauser
Texas Instruments	Williams Companies
Texas Utilities	Xerox

Source: Labor Policy Association 1993.

in the union-management forums of the more liberal and research-oriented National Planning Association.) Few prominent executives appear willing to dissociate themselves completely from the hard-line politics of the LPA. In the final analysis, it may be that most employers, even those formally committed to collective bargaining, want to retain the option to participate in anti-union offensives.

The LPA's role with regard to the Teamwork for Employees and Managers (TEAM) Act, an effort to weaken the Wagner Act ban on company unions, demonstrates the organization's commitment to a largely union-free economy. The House of Representatives passed the TEAM Act on September 27, 1995, by 221 to 202. The Senate also approved the measure by a vote of 53 to 46 on July 10, 1996, but it was then vetoed by President Clinton. Advocates have argued that the TEAM Act represents only a technical change in Section 8(a)(2), permitting employee involvement in non-union settings. Since the enactment of the Wagner Act in 1935, U.S. labor law has outlawed company unions, management-controlled organizations offering the illusion of employee voice (and the reality of employer surveillance), in order to guarantee employee rights to organization and collective bargaining. Although proponents insist that advancing legitimate employee involvement plans is the objective of this measure, it would almost certainly hasten the decline of organized labor.

According to the advocates of the TEAM Act, the vast majority of American employers now recognize the value of employee involvement in decision making. They assert that employee involvement, by which they mean management-sponsored structures for discussions concerning workplace matters, is critical to international competitiveness. Former Representative Steven Gunderson offered these comments in the floor debate:

Members have all heard about total quality management, they have heard about quality circles, they have heard about quality of life, quality of work programs, self-directed work teams, productivity teams, and all the like. As we try to deal with these issues to be competitive in an international arena, it is essential that in nonunion settings they may occur without being a violation of law. (*Congressional Record* 1995a)

Recent decisions of the NLRB, primarily *Electromation* and *DuPont*, have stimulated employer concern with the implementation of Section 8(a)(2). In *Electromation*, the Board ruled that management-sponsored action committees, which ostensibly were created to deal with worker dissatisfaction with wages and other terms of employment, constituted a labor organization under management domination. In *DuPont*, the Board ruled that DuPont's creation of a safety committee under its own control (after having refused to negotiate with its union about one) was an unfair labor practice. Both cases appear to involve management strategies to block independent representation for workers.

The LPA played a crucial role in drafting the TEAM Act and now coordinates much of the work of anti-union employers in their effort to overhaul labor law. The LPA submitted *amicus curiae* briefs in support of Electromation and DuPont before the NLRB, and it argued strenuously for reform of 8(a)(2) before the Dunlop Commission on the Future of Worker-Management Relations and in every other available forum.

It is noteworthy that Congressional advocates of the TEAM Act opposed the Moran (Democrat-Virginia) amendment which would have required that any employee committee members be selected by the free choice of employees. For example, Representative Harris Fawell (Republican-Illinois) commented: "I also have to oppose the [Moran] amendment, the concept of introducing an election into this area of voluntary employee teams ... what we would be doing now is to introduce the concept of an election, and that in turn raises all kinds of questions" (*Congressional Record* 1995b).

One reason why LPA leaders want no requirement of elections is that it might stimulate unionism or its equivalent: independent worker representation. Employers want nothing that reminds employees of unionism.

Although the LPA insists that Section 8(a)(2) (as interpreted by the *Electromation* and *DuPont* decisions of the NLRB) blocks employee involvement programs, other human resource professionals disagree. Joseph Bacarro, chief executive of ActionTakers in Kansas City, Kansas, and a member of the Society for Human Resource Management's Employee and Labor Relations Committee, has argued that the disbandment of company-sponsored worker committees is no reason for employers to abandon quality initiatives. In an article by Stephenie Overman in *HR News*, Bacarro observes:

Companies that want to look for an out can use the [*DuPont*] decision as an excuse. But the decision doesn't say that they can't have committees as problem-solving tools. . . . The troubles come when [companies] try to make the teams representative [of the workers]. . . . That's traditionally the union's role. (Overman 1994, p. A7)

LPA representatives themselves found no obstacle in existing labor law to the development of "joint participation programs giving employees and union representatives a greater voice in management decision-making" in a report provided to the Department of Labor in 1987 (Scott 1995). They would probably explain that the *Electromation* and *DuPont* rulings of the NLRB generated the threats to employee involvement that the LPA now proposes to correct with the TEAM Act. However, the *amicus curiae* briefs filed by the LPA on behalf of Electromation and DuPont were clearly designed to persuade the Board to liberally rein- terpret (even to change) labor law to permit Electroma- tion's "Action Committees" and DuPont's unilaterally- established safety committees to stand despite Section 8(a)(2).

Leaders of the LPA feel that they have been unfairly dis- advantaged for years by the power of pro-labor Democrats on the House and Senate Labor Committees. They were annoyed by the modest union sympathies of the Dunlop Commission on the Future of Worker-Management Rela- tions (appointed by Labor Secretary Reich). They viewed the Republican conquest of Congress as an unusual oppor- tunity to advance their "long-frustrated" agenda. They would like to deliver a final blow to a weakened labor move- ment and its allies in the Democratic party. The LPA and Congressional Republicans want, at a minimum, to permit Electromation, DuPont, and other firms to define the state of the art in company unionism.

In 1995, Jeffrey McGuiness endeavored to quash what he regarded as a threatening movement of academics. Pro- fessors Hoyt Wheeler at the University of South Carolina, Harry Katz at Cornell University, and Clyde Summers at the University of Pennsylvania circulated a petition in op- position to the LPA-backed TEAM Act in the spring of 1995. In an April 18 letter to LPA members, McGuiness warned, "Academics Mobilize to Block Employee Involve- ment." He laid particular stress on the involvement of fac- ulty at Cornell's School of Industrial and Labor Relations in the petition drive, noting that "several LPA members have close ties with [the School]." The McGuiness letter left the false impression that Cornell itself sponsored the peti- tion drive. McGuiness' note stimulated a letter-writing campaign from LPA vice presidents for human resources to Katz, Wheeler, and Summers and their institutions. Some letters charged the faculty with poor scholarship, bias, and inaccuracy, predicting that their students would find no jobs. Several LPA member corporations are major contributors to research institutes at the School of Industrial and Labor Relations and the Wharton School. The harshness of the LPA rhetoric suggested that some corporate members view academic freedom as an obstacle to their advocacy role. (Clearly, the free expression of faculty is not a form of employee involvement that LPA members value.)

The LPA's *amicus curiae* briefs reveal the authoritarian model of labor relations that underlies all that the LPA does. While McGuiness and others at the LPA proclaim their commitment to humane forms of employee involvement, the policies they advocate have the primary effect of enhancing the powers of managers. When Town and Country Electric and Ameristaff Personnel Contractors, Ltd., appealed a decision of the NLRB upholding the protected employee status of paid union organizers ("salts"), an LPA brief that supported these companies presupposed an unrealistic model of employee subservience. How is one to reconcile traditional notions of servant status with employee involvement? (Williams and Yager 1995).

Jeff McGuiness has long characterized William Gould, retiring chair of the National Labor Relations Board (NLRB), as a stooge of organized labor. Gould's varied experience (as an arbitrator, NLRB staffer, management lawyer, and UAW counsel) has lent credence to his claims of neutrality. He sought for years to avoid compromise of his reputation to maintain his credibility as an arbitrator. Although critical of many management practices in his book *Agenda for Reform* (Gould 1993), he severely criticized unions' racial policies in *Black Workers and White Unions* (Gould 1977). Nevertheless, an LPA report prior to his confirmation warned that Gould would attempt to enforce his own views on replacement workers through covert manipulation of Board policy. Apparently, Gould's clear commitment to collective bargaining was sufficient to convict him in McGuiness' eyes. During Gould's service as NLRB chair (beginning in 1993), the Board's willingness to pursue 10–J injunctions against employers repeatedly committing unfair labor practices has provoked LPA condemnation (*Daily Labor Report* 1994b).

In 1997, the LPA mounted a major new campaign to discredit the Board under Gould's leadership, publishing a diatribe entitled *NLRB: Agency in Crisis* (Yager 1997). Author Dan Yager charges that the NLRB has lost all impartiality, providing as evidence its adverse rulings involving Caterpillar and Overnite Express, both of which have been consistent labor law violators. Apparently, Yager and his colleagues at the LPA believe impartiality in labor relations to require warm acceptance of union-busting.

As a show of support for Caterpillar's anti-union drive (in which the firm threatened to permanently replace its strikers and disciplined union members for wearing shirts and buttons with messages critical of the company), McGuiness denounced John Calhoun Wells, the current Director of the Federal Mediation and Conciliation Service. Wells, who was attempting to mediate the UAW-Caterpillar dispute in 1994, apparently had endorsed the principle of a Kennedy-Metzenbaum measure to prohibit the hiring of permanent replacements in written correspondence with the senators. McGuiness asserted that:

all agency officials are employed with the requirement that they maintain strict neutrality on political and public policy matters that come before the agency. We are concerned that because of your endorsement of the legislation, employers may no longer view the Service as able to carry out its mission.

A spokeswoman for Wells countered: "[Wells'] response was pro-collective bargaining. It was neither pro-labor, nor pro-management. It is his job and responsibility to promote collective bargaining and sound, stable labor relations. That's what he is doing."

It is not particularly surprising that Wells, a Clinton appointee, would lend his support to a measure the administration had endorsed. McGuiness apparently hoped to discredit Wells in order to advance the Caterpillar cause. More broadly, McGuiness' objective was to protect the right of all employers to hire permanent replacements (*Daily Labor Report* 1994a).

McGuiness demonstrated his view of the limits of professional independence in his efforts to punish the American College of Occupational and Environmental Medicine (ACOEM) in its moment of courage. In 1994, the ACOEM was initially supportive of the AFL-CIO–backed Comprehensive Occupational Safety and Health Reform Act, which would have, among other things, required the formation of safety committees in firms of at least eleven employees. The ACOEM includes among its members many corporate medical directors. McGuiness revealed in an interview with the *National Journal* that he had alerted the Washington Representatives of LPA corporations to the possibility that their medical directors had advanced labor's approach to OSHA reform. The ACOEM withdrew its endorsement (Victor 1994).

The LPA's John Tysse has played a leadership role in the Coalition on Occupational Safety and Health, an employer group that was founded to combat the AFL-CIO efforts to improve the enforcement of the Occupational Safety and Health Act and which now leads the campaign to weaken the law. In 1994, an LPA ally, Representative Cass Ballenger (Republican-North Carolina), introduced a reform measure that would limit the Occupational Safety and Health Administration to a largely advisory role and weaken the general duty clause of the Act. This provision had been the legal basis for fines on employers whose employees suffered from cumulative trauma disorders. Tysse's Coalition drafted the Ballenger bill in the Washington boardroom of the National Association of Manufacturers, with substantial input from the lobbyist of the United Parcel Service, an LPA member firm.

Herbert Northrup, a Wharton School professor and former General Electric strategist, has played an important role in the LPA's activities of the last three decades by helping to develop tactics and providing research support (through the Industrial Research Unit and its affiliate, the Research Advisory Group, at the Wharton School). Northrup brought to LPA the practical experience he had acquired in labor relations at GE, where he helped develop "Boulwarism," or "take-it-or-leave-it" bargaining.

Many of the reports published by the Industrial Research Unit had been commissioned by the LPA. Northrup assisted the LPA in its campaign for greater political influence. Prior to the 1960s, the employer organization was perceived by many practitioners and policymakers to be little more than an instrument of southern reaction. The Wharton professor solidified the LPA's connections to major American corporations as well as to the Republican party, through his recommendation that Ken McGuiness, a party strategist on labor issues, assume leadership of the Association.[1]

Writer Jonathan Rosenblum argues in *Copper Crucible* (Rosenblum 1995, 60–63) that the Industrial Research Unit played a critical role in the decision by Phelps Dodge to hire permanent replacements to break a strike in 1983. In 1982, the Wharton institute had published a report entitled *Operating During Strikes*, which provided detailed instructions for anti-union offensives. Phelps Dodge was a founding member of the euphemistically-labeled Research Advisory Group and apparently provided the first test of the book's recommendations.

BOULWARISM

The philosophy of the LPA and allied business lobbies is well represented in miniature by "Boulwarism." Bloom and Northrup (1981, p. 126) provide this definition and justification for Boulwarism:

Dissatisfaction with the "haggling" approach to collective bargaining has induced some employers to come to the bargaining table with a carefully researched and thought-out proposal, offer it to the union, and at the same time announce it to the employees. The bargaining offensive in this instance reverts to the employer, and the bargaining which does occur usually concerns possible or minor modifications in the company offer.... This approach has been utilized with great success by a few large companies. It is known as "Boulwarism," after L. R. Boulware, a former vice president of General Electric Company, who publicized it widely.

Bloom and Northrup fail to note the NLRB's determination that Boulwarism constitutes an illegal failure to bargain in good faith in this passage.

Boulware himself described GE's approach in this manner:

In short, General Electric's policy—of trying its level best at all times, to do voluntarily in the balanced-best-interests of all—was no pious posing for cheap publicity but was a constant one-jump-ahead-of-the-sheriff necessity in order first to survive and then, hopefully, to grow in that usefulness to all which was the clear opportunity if all the interested parties cooperated toward such usefulness. (1969, p. 30)

Boulware's book, *The Truth about Boulwarism: Trying to Do Right Voluntarily* (1969), provides appeals to industrial harmony paradoxically combined with attacks on those interests that might challenge management.

In Boulware's mind, American business was everywhere beset by perils. Government bureaucrats were determined to impose a socialist system. Communist militants and their allies were in control of trade unions. Boulware was confident, however, that individual workers and consumers could be persuaded to abandon the distorted view of business that he believed labor leaders and radicals promoted. He was deeply committed to economic education programs for GE's workers. Classes for workers and supervisors, posters, and mailings to all employees were elements of Boulware's economic education strategy, designed to reinforce the philosophy of free enterprise.

In much of his own writing, Boulware stressed the notion of "contributor-claimant," which was his name for each of the groups: workers, consumers, stockholders, and others who were parties to GE's economic activity. In this argument, he anticipated modern debate concerning the relationship of management to "stakeholders." He submitted that GE's unified approach to labor relations, community relations, and consumer relations satisfied the "balanced-best-interest" of all. Boulware hired Ronald Reagan and served as his mentor in the 1950s, as Reagan addressed consumers and workers, proclaiming GE's beneficence and modernity. Reagan provided a genial face for Boulwarism inside and outside GE (Saloma 1984).

Boulware's concept of justice was rooted in the 1940s status quo at GE. Power was nowhere evident in his analysis, only the alleged harmony of market processes and the sensitivity of a company that understood its consumers' and employees' wants. Boulware's corporate strategy of "intimate authoritarianism" is surely consistent with all that the LPA demands.

"Facts" were, in Boulware's analysis, merely reflections of the underlying truths of economics. (He went so far as to argue that the Great Depression was a misconception of the newspapers and an excuse for the mistaken policies of the New Deal.) While Boulware believed that ordinary workers were capable of understanding economics, he was certain that elite/managerial guidance was crucial.

In a letter to E. Wight Bakke at Yale University, Boulware denied having read any critical essays on "Boulwarism":

> You may find it hard to believe that I don't read these articles about so-called "Boulwareism," but the flood of them has been so great for twelve years, and the sameness of their repeating unwarranted charges of non-existent malfeasance on our part has been so pronounced, that the library long ago ceased sending me anything unless it contained something new or significantly interesting. I believe greatly in learning most from those who disagree, but there got to be nothing new in these attacks.[2]

Boulware's dogmatism and disdain for his critics are evident in this letter. In fact, there is even a touch of Boulwarism in his claim that he was willing to learn from his critics, just as GE management insisted that it would alter its bargaining proposals only in the light of new "facts."

THE EMPLOYMENT POLICY FOUNDATION

The Employment Policy Foundation is the research arm of the LPA. The Foundation's 1995 book, *Keeping America Competitive* (Potter and Youngman 1995), reveals the underlying logic of LPA demands. (See an excerpt in the documentary appendix.) Although the authors boast of the innovative work practices of the modern corporation, their emphasis upon "competitiveness" and rejection of "one-size-fits-all" regulation promises worst-practice businesses the freedom to match low standards elsewhere in the world. The several hundred pages of rhetoric include many other anti-worker proposals that Republicans have introduced to this session of Congress. For example, the volume recommends legislation for greater flexibility in the administration of the Fair Labor Standards Act, ostensibly to accommodate family needs; the likely result would be the demise of the forty-hour work week. The Employment Policy Foundation and LPA also favor the repeal of the Davis-Bacon law mandating prevailing wages on federal construction projects.

The LPA/EPF program is informed by an admixture of naive optimism and manipulative cynicism. Theologian Reinhold Niebuhr wrote of the children of light and the children of darkness. The children of light incorrectly assume that human nature is perfectible (Niebuhr 1944, p. 118). The leaders of LPA/EPF are children of light in that they argue that the managers of the largest American corporations on the whole do good despite the temptation to abuse their great power. (Niebuhr warned, "Inordinate power tempts its holders to abuse it, which means to use it for their own ends.") These managers must at times be aware of the potential (and everyday) abuse of corporate power, that they are implicitly sanctioning plant shutdowns to avoid unionism and purchasing products from sweatshops, among other questionable acts. Here they join the children of darkness "who know no law beyond their will and interest" (Niebuhr 1944, p. 9).

The LPA/EPF has always sought consensus among large employers on human resource issues, but it is a consensus driven by fundamentalist employers with scant attention given to sophisticated conservatives or liberals. By definition, sophisticated conservatives and liberals in the business community embrace a philosophy that promises concessions to non-business constituencies. In the LPA/EPF calculus, such concessions distract employers from the defense of their own interests.

The LPA, of course, is not the only business lobby in Washington, nor is it the most important. However, in the emerging division of labor among lobbies on the right, the LPA plays a critical role in coordinating efforts among employers to lift the constraints on managers' unilateral authority. The varied membership of the Association's board of directors demonstrates that the LPA has broad support among American employers.

In the period immediately following World War II, there were many employers who appreciated the notions that sales depend upon consumers' income, that consumers' income depends upon adequate wages, that collective bargaining serves society by boosting wages, and that compliance with federal regulation is a reasonable cost of doing business. The ideology that guides the Labor Policy Association is, of course, very different. The LPA favors the unconstrained, unilateral authority of managers and it apparently will brook no compromise with organized labor. (The industrial relations of the non-union, "business-friendly" southern United States may meet the requirements of the LPA program.) The support the LPA enjoys from leading American corporations underscores how difficult it would be to forge grand compromises between business and labor, of the sort that John Dunlop sought as chairman of the Commission on the Future of Worker-Management Relations.

EXCERPT FROM KEEPING AMERICA COMPETITIVE FROM EMPLOYMENT POLICY FOUNDATION

EMPLOYMENT POLICY PRINCIPLES

Rapid intercontinental transportation, instant telecommunications, and worldwide diffusion of technologies have eliminated or diminished many competitive advantages enjoyed by American industry in the decades following World War II. As the twenty-first century approaches, we can no longer assume that America will win the competitive race by reason of superior technology or mass production capability. In the global marketplace, American economic competitiveness will depend in large measure upon how well we prepare and harness our nation's human resources.

American employment policies and laws today are made, however, with little consideration for how they affect American competitiveness. U.S. employment laws usually are enacted in an adversarial, emotionally charged atmosphere, with government, business, organized labor, and other special interests all pulling in different directions. Employers have sought to retain flexibility to adapt to changes in the marketplace and workplace, while government and employee groups have focused upon protecting individuals from change by imposing new regulations and mandates on employers. In this contest between employers seeking flexibility and others seeking specific protections for individuals, the latter usually carries the day. The result over the last three decades has been an explosion in new workplace legal restrictions backed up by the threat of litigation and increasingly severe remedies.

What rarely has been considered in this policymaking process is how individuals ultimately are affected by employment law restrictions and mandates that, separately or cumulatively, make U.S. businesses less competitive in the global economy. For example:

At what point does the creation of new workplace rights and remedies enforceable by the threat of litigation force employers to adopt personnel policies and practices so defensive in nature that they begin to undermine trust and cooperation in the workplace?

At what point is the value to employees of another new workplace protection outweighed by the detriment to other individuals, and/or to our economy as a whole, in lost job opportunities resulting from the inability of U.S. companies to continue to absorb additional labor costs or to operate efficiently in the face of further workplace restrictions?

At what point does the added cost of yet another mandated benefit force employers to cut wages, defer wage increases, or eliminate other benefits that many employees might value more highly than the newly mandated one?

Policymakers generally have been unconcerned about these questions. But as Americans increasingly seek to understand why their traditional jobs and industries are disappearing, why their real wages are growing only slowly, why the quality of their work lives seems to be deteriorating, and why their standard of living is not rising as rapidly as it did in earlier decades, these are questions that must be addressed.

America must reassess its employment laws and policies in light of the new competitive realities and rules of the game that our nation faces on the eve of the twenty-first century. We must better balance competitive and social policy needs and goals. Our employment policies must be consistent with the convergence of marketplace, technological, workplace, and work force changes that are redefining American employer-employee relations, the workplace, and the nature of work itself.

We believe that six employment policy principles and goals should guide policymakers in reevaluating and revising existing laws and policies to better promote the competitiveness of American companies and the interests of their employees:

Principle No. 1

A primary goal of U.S. employment policy should be to preserve and enhance the ability of American companies to create and provide jobs. The economic security and well-being of American workers depends first and foremost on the availability of jobs. Policy measures intended to benefit employees may cause more harm than good if they add excessively to the costs of providing employment, or impede the ability of American companies to compete successfully in the global marketplace.

Principle No. 2

Proposed changes in employment laws and policies should be assessed in the context of America's economic and competitiveness objectives. Policymakers should begin viewing employment policies in conjunction with related trade policies, public and private investment policies, and overall regulatory policies that also affect competitiveness. Employment policies should not be developed looking exclusively at social policy objectives.

The effects of employment policies include not only direct costs but also the indirect effects of the policy on costs of doing business and on employers' flexibility, adaptability, responsiveness to change, and other competitive factors. Policymakers should consider not only the individual costs and effects of each new policy proposal, but also assess how it would add to the total burden that government restrictions and mandates place on the competitiveness of American employers and employees.

Principle No. 3

Employment policies should be based on an accurate understanding of current conditions and practices in American workplaces. Employers and employees alike suffer under the weight of too many generalized legal restrictions and requirements enacted to address exceptional situations. The maxim that "hard cases make bad law" is too often true, whether the law is made in the courts, in the regulatory agencies, or by legislatures. Policymakers should take account of the wide variation, not only of America's population and work force, but also of its business structures and forms of workplace organization. Rigid, "one-size-fits-all" requirements and assumptions should be avoided in favor of flexible approaches that foster experimentation, innovation, and adaptation.

Principle No. 4

Workplace policies, procedures, and requirements should, to the greatest extent practicable, be developed and implemented at the local or company level by those most directly affected. Solutions developed by the persons immediately involved tend to fit problems better. Locally designed solutions are likely to have fewer unforeseen adverse consequences than ones imposed by government officials or other outsiders who are less familiar with the facts and circumstances of a particular workplace and have no personal stake in making sure the solutions work.

Principle No. 5

Workplace laws and regulations should be written so as to allow flexibility in the achievement of defined policy goals. Public policy objectives can be achieved in a wide variety of ways. To preserve workplace flexibility, laws and regulations should be no more prescriptive than is necessary. They should clearly define the essential ends to be met, but should, as far as possible, leave it up to the parties immediately involved to decide upon the specific ways of meeting those ultimate objectives.

Rigid insistence on overly prescriptive processes often unnecessarily impedes flexibility and wastes resources of both employers and government compliance officials. Employers whose programs and practices meet the objectives of public policy should not be penalized by an approach that exalts form over substance. Paperwork requirements should be minimized. Where reports and recordkeeping are unavoidable, they should be structured to minimize the paperwork burden on employers.

Principle No. 6

Employment laws and public policies should be consistent and non-duplicative. Although it is desirable that employers and government enforcement officials have flexibility to tailor policies and solutions to varying circumstances in individual cases, the imposition of conflicting or inconsistent general rules or mandates by different branches of government (federal, state, or local), or by different agencies or officials within the same government, is counterproductive and anti-competitive. To the extent that mandates are necessary, they should be consistent so that employers doing business in multiple jurisdictions can maintain uniform policies and records where it is desirable and efficient to do so.

NOTES

1. Interviews with principals of the Industrial Research Unit (now called the Center for Human Resources), Wharton School, University of Pennsylvania, Philadelphia, Pennsylvania, November 8, 1995.

2. Letter from Lemuel Boulware to E. Wight Bakke, August 25, 1959, Box 32, Folder 757, Lemuel Boulware papers, University of Pennsylvania.

REFERENCES

Bloom, G. F., and H. R. Northrup. (1981). *Economics of labor relations*. 9th ed. Homewood, Ill.: Richard D. Irwin, Inc.

Boulware, L. R. (1969). *The truth about Boulwarism: Trying to do right voluntarily*. Washington, D.C.: Bureau of National Affairs.

Congressional Record. (1995a). September 27: H9523.

Congressional Record. (1995b). September 27: H9549.

Daily Labor Report. (1994a). June 21, p. D13.

Daily Labor Report. (1994b). January 28, p. D3.

Gould, W. L. (1993). *Agenda for reform*. Cambridge, Mass.: MIT Press.

———. (1977). *Black workers in white unions*. Ithaca, N.Y.: Cornell University Press.

Labor Policy Association. (1993). *Annual Report*. Washington, D.C.

Levitan, S., and M. Cooper (1985). *Business lobbies: The public good and the bottom line*. Baltimore, Md.: Johns Hopkins University Press.

Niebuhr, R. (1944). *The children of light and the children of darkness*. New York: Scribner's.

Overman, S. (1994). "NLRB disbands DuPont's worker committees." *HR News* (July 12): p. A7.

Potter, E. E., and J. A. Youngman. (1995). *Keeping America competitive: Employment policy for the twenty-first century*. Lakewood, Colo.: Glenbridge Publishing.

Rosenblum, J. D. (1995). *Copper crucible*. Ithaca, N.Y.: ILR Press.

Saloma III, J. S. (1984). *Ominous politics: The new conservative labyrinth*. New York: Hill and Wang.

Scott, J. (1995). Testimony by Judith Scott, Teamsters General Counsel, before Subcommittee on Employer-Employee Relations of House Committee on Economic and Educational Opportunities, February 8.

Victor, K. (1994). "Delivering the corporate counterpunch." *National Journal* (April 16): 909.

Williams, R. E. and D. V. Yager of McGuiness and Williams. (1995). Brief before Supreme Court in support of employers' position on appeal from Eighth Circuit (*Town and Country Electric Inc. v. NLRB*, 34 F.3rd 625, 629 [8th Cir. 1994]).

Yager, D. V. (1997). *NLRB: Agency in crisis.* Washington, D.C.: Labor Policy Association.

Case Studies: Health Care Reform and Occupational Disease Notification

HEALTH CARE REFORM

While many trade unions have long supported national health insurance (and the Nixon administration favored employer mandates), major business lobbies have ordinarily been hostile to such an extension of government control. Unions, including the UAW, and major corporations, including General Motors, have in recent decades faced the problem of rising health care costs, particularly in collectively bargained health plans. Labor has pressed the employers for endorsement of national health insurance (in negotiations with employer representatives and within joint panels like John Dunlop's private Labor-Management Group in the 1970s). As late as the 1970s, General Motors remained unprepared to break with business orthodoxy on health care reform. However, in the late 1980s, some employers providing generous health plans responded to rising premiums by reconsidering their doubts about governmental solutions (Jacobs 1987, 1989).

Discussions among leaders of business and labor led to the formation of the National Leadership Coalition for Health Care Reform. This organization includes executives from Chrysler, Bethlehem Steel, Cincinnati Bell, Dayton-Hudson, Georgia-Pacific, International Paper, Lockheed, Safeway, Xerox, and other corporations. They endorsed a modified mandated benefits approach, according to which employers would be required either to provide health insurance to their employees or pay a payroll tax for a government plan. The Leadership Coalition was joined by the Health Care Reform Project, which specifically endorsed the Clinton health care reform initiative in 1994. This latter organization approached reform with a greater sense of urgency, and received support from three businesses: American Airlines, Chrysler, and Southern California Edison. Small businesses unhappy with the hostile reaction of the National Federation of Independent Business (NFIB) to reform joined the Small Business Health Care Reform Coalition, which was organized to counter the NFIB's doctrinaire stance (with support from the American Booksellers Association, National Farmers Union, National Farmers Organization, the National Retail Druggists Association, and other groups) (Jacobs 1989).

Despite apparently increasing business support for health care reform, the Business Roundtable (BR) deferred to the interests of health-related companies[1] and chose to oppose the Clinton administration bill that would mandate employer provision of health benefits. CEOs of General Motors, Ford, Chrysler Corporation, Bethlehem Steel, American Airlines, Southern California Edison, and other firms voted in favor of the Clinton plan within a BR committee. Seventeen of the sixty-five companies participating in the vote represented health-related businesses.[2]

When the Chamber of Commerce showed some openness to the Clinton administration's budget proposals early in 1994, Republican party leaders in Congress reacted with an anger and hostility that revealed their assumptions about the Chamber's relationship to them. Some of the officers of the organization had at first been sympathetic to the concept of employer mandates, which led to consternation within Republican Congressional circles. The GOP placed pressure on the Chamber leadership and helped mobilize grassroots members of the Chamber. In apparent response, the Chamber withdrew conciliatory testimony on Clinton's health bill prepared for a Congressional committee (Rich and Devroy 1994).

Representatives of the National Federation of Independent Business, the National Restaurant Association, the National Retail Federation, Kmart, McDonald's, J. C. Penney, Marriott, and other large service sector enterprises formed the Anti-Mandate Coalition in 1994. The group's apparent strategy was to have conservative small business activists publicly argue the case against employer mandates, and declare their economic vulnerability, while far wealthier businesses more quietly fought for the right to deny health insurance to their employees. NFIB legislative director John Motley said, "I see us ... the business community ... in a position of controlling between 55 and 60 votes in the Senate." The NFIB spent two-thirds of its annual budget in 1994 in its effort to defeat any employer mandates (Lewis 1994).

More privately, an alliance of conservative groups (e.g., the Christian Coalition, the National Taxpayers Union, and business lobbies), calling themselves the "No Name Coalition," met frequently to plot strategy to defeat health care reform. The No Name Coalition played a role in the Chamber's apparent reversal on the Clinton measure (Johnson and Broder 1996, pp. 53, 197, 323).

Senator Edward Kennedy (Democrat-Massachusetts) and other supporters of the Clinton plan brought Pizza Hut into the public debate by charging that Pizza Hut (and

McDonald's) prospered in Germany and Japan where they were required to insure their employees while opposing employer mandates in the United States. Members of Congress cited a report from the Health Care Reform Project. Pizza Hut was able to persuade four Washington, D.C. television stations to refuse to carry a Project advertisement charging Pizza Hut with hypocrisy. (The company is based in Kansas, and both of Kansas' Republican senators, Robert Dole and Nancy Kassebaum, rushed to denounce the ad.) (Priest 1994; Clymer 1994) (Other anti-reform groups included the Healthcare Equity Action League and the National Business Coalition on Health.)

Ameritech executives received a sharp rebuke from the Republican leadership for their endorsement of health care reform. Michael Weisskopf noted in the *Washington Post*, "Four Republicans on the [House] Energy and Commerce subcommittee on telecommunications and finance, including the ranking minority member, wrote Ameritech President Richard C. Notebaert registering 'strong displeasure' with the endorsement and pointedly referring to pending industry legislation vital to the company" (Weisskopf 1994b). Firms supporting the Health Care Reform Project faced considerable informal protest from other businesses.

Writer John Judis (1995) laments the failed opportunity for health care reform in Clinton's first term and notes business interest in reform. However, he does not perceive the obstructionist role played by mainstream business lobbies and the substantial pressure brought to bear against business advocates of reform.

OCCUPATIONAL DISEASE NOTIFICATION

In the 100th Congress (1987–1988), the Chamber of Commerce, National Association of Manufacturers, National Federation of Business and other business lobbies cooperated with the Reagan administration to defeat the High Risk Occupational Disease Notification and Prevention Act. The purpose of the measure was to establish a twenty-five million dollar federal program to identify, notify, and provide medical monitoring of workers who have been exposed to toxic substances in the workplace. The federal government would bear the responsibility for notifying at-risk employees, and employers would be obliged to pay for the monitoring of employees who were exposed to toxic chemicals on the job. The bill was the result of negotiations between the AFL-CIO and General Electric, the American Electronics Association, and the Chemical Manufacturers Association. A team of specialists at General Electric had carefully evaluated early drafts of the legislation and had recommended changes to a receptive Senator Metzenbaum (Democrat-Ohio), chairman of the Senate Labor subcommittee. Industry groups sought and won a provision in the bill that would deny workers the ability to sue employers based on notice received under the bill.[3]

Despite substantial business involvement in the development of the bill, the Chamber of Commerce, the National Federation of Independent Business, the Labor Policy Association, the American Hotel and Motel Association, and other business groups were in opposition. Opponents charged that the measure would encourage frivolous litigation against employers even where workers were exposed to essentially safe chemicals. Pro-business product liability lobbyist Victor E. Schwartz wrote, "the High Risk Bill will trigger new workers' compensation and tort liability claims against employers, and products liability lawsuits against businesses and manufacturers of products used in the workplace" (Schwartz 1989, p. 106).

The Employment Policy Foundation, a tax-exempt research affiliate of the Labor Policy Association, sponsored a study (by Robert Nathan Associates) of proposed legislation for mandated health insurance, plant closing notification, family leave, and occupational disease notification. The study found that the four measures together might cost 100 billion dollars yearly. The 1993 Labor Policy Association annual report claims that this study was a "significant factor in the defeat of the risk notification and mandated health bills" (Labor Policy Association 1993, p. 42).

Occupational disease notification was ultimately defeated by a filibuster in the Senate led by Senators Orrin Hatch (Republican-Utah) and Dan Quayle (Republican-Indiana) after four unsuccessful attempts at cloture. While the Chemical Manufacturers Association and other trade associations engaged in good-faith bargaining on this issue (recognizing that liability lawsuits would occur even in the absence of legislation and that court cases often turned on the employers' failure to inform employees of serious risks on the job), conservative Republicans and mainstream business lobbies opposed any compromise with the AFL-CIO. The NFIB waged an extremely effective letter-writing campaign. The Washington representatives for General Electric and the American Electronics Association endured considerable abuse from Congressional Republicans and the business community for their support of the high risk measure. (Senator Quayle urged the CEO of GE to fire Washington counsel Martin Conner.)[4]

Senator John Breaux (Democrat-Louisiana) complained:

Despite all we have done in addressing the reasons why people said they are not for the bill, no matter what we do, I am afraid the other side would never accept this legislation. . . . I received an interesting letter from the Secretary of Labor [Lynn Martin] saying they are adamantly opposed to this bill, that it is so seriously flawed that the bill cannot be amended so as to be acceptable. (Breaux 1989, pp. 122, 124)

Remarks in the Senate debate by Senator Hatch (Republican-Utah) reveal his immense displeasure that major business organizations had embraced the high risk measure. He charged:

I happen to know that a large number of Chemical Manufacturers Association members are very upset that one of the, to use their terms, knuckleheads at the head of that organization have [*sic*] indicated any kind of support to this. And of course the American Electronics Association, there are also a lot of upset people there who do not agree with what the national association has done. You go down to the National Paint and Coatings Association. My goodness, there is a lot of dissent in these organizations, and rightly so. (*Congressional Record* 1988, S2834)

On the other hand, Senator Metzenbaum (Democrat-Ohio) noted business support with pleasure and perhaps some amazement, and described an apparent business backlash:

The fact is a major segment of the business community supports the legislation. In all my years as a legislator, including my days in the Ohio Senate and the Ohio General Assembly, I have never seen such a broad coalition of support for legislation to help workers. . . . You turn around and look at this chart that is behind us, and there you find about 29 separate health and environmental supporters of S. 79, including the Chemical Manufacturers Association, whose members account for over 90% of the chemicals generated in the United States, the American Electronics Association, with over 3,000 member companies, the National Paint and Coatings Association, with over 1,000 member companies, Crum and Forster Insurance Cos., the second largest property and casualty insurers in the country, Atlantic Richfield, Occidental Petroleum . . . and so many more, including the one company that has experienced more than any other company in America the hazards of occupational illnesses, formerly the Johns-Manville Corp., now known as the Manville Corp. (*Congressional Record* 1988, S2768)

Since business support surfaced for S.79, there has been a fierce, and well-orchestrated, attack on the companies and associations who decided to support the bill. It is not surprising that a handful of CMA [Chemical Manufacturers Association] members decided to disassociate themselves from CMA's position in light of these strong attacks. Several of the seven companies who changed their mind are primarily involved in other industries and have stronger ties to other trade associations. This is true of Philips Petroleum and Oil, Eli Lilly ... Georgia Pacific and Paper Products. Perhaps they could not take the heat. (*Congressional Record* 1988, S2771)

The elections of 1986 had resulted in a Democratic majority in the Senate. The tragedy at Union Carbide in Bhopal, India, had exposed the chemical industry to public criticism. Apparently, many chemical and electronics executives perceived that compromise with liberal forces was now expedient. The prospect of acceleration of action by a Democratic Congress on social legislation persuaded some business lobbyists that failure to compromise would marginalize them. Worker notification of chemical hazards was appealing to some companies because it might be a defense against corporate liability. On the other hand, a trade association deal with organized labor and liberal Democrats was an extremely disturbing prospect both to mainstream business lobbies and to Republicans (at the grassroots and in Congress).

NOTES

1. Insurance companies have sought to influence the debate over health care reform through two lobbies: the Health Insurance Association of America (representing smaller insurers) and the Alliance for Managed Competition (for the larger firms).

2. Phone interview with Martin Conner, former Washington Counsel, General Electric, August 24, 1994.

3. Phone interview with James Brudney, former staff director for the Labor Subcommittee of the Senate Labor and Human Resources Committee, August 22, 1994.

4. Phone interview with Martin Conner, former Washington Counsel, General Electric, August 24, 1994.

REFERENCES

Breaux, J. (1989). "Should the Congress adopt the 'high-risk occupational disease negotiation and prevention act of 1987.' Pro." *Congressional Digest* 68, no. 4 (April): 122, 124.

Clymer, A. (1994). "Pizza Hut blocks group's ad about health insurance practices." *New York Times* (July 16): A1.

Congressional Record. (1988). March 22: S2768, S2771, S2834.

Flemming, A. S., and E. L. Richardson. (1994). "Let the employers provide." *Washington Post* (June 12): C7.

Jacobs, D. C. (1987). "The UAW and the Committee for National Health Insurance: The contours of social unionism." In D. Lewin, D. B. Lipsky, and D. Sockell (eds.), *Advances in industrial and labor relations*. Greenwich, Conn.: JAI Press Inc., 4: 119–140.

———. (1989). "Labor and the strategy of mandated health benefits." *Labor Studies Journal* 14, no. 3: 23–33.

Johnson, H., and D. S. Broder. (1996). *The system: The American way of politics at the breaking point*. Boston: Little, Brown and Co.

Judis, J. B. (1995). "Abandoned surgery: Business and the failure of health care reform." *American Prospect* 21 (Spring): 65–73.

Labor Policy Association. (1993). *Annual report*. Washington, D.C.: Labor Policy Association.

Lewis, C. (1994). "In sickness and in wealth: How a swarm of lobbyists cornered the debate on health care reform." *Washington Post* (August 21): C2.

Mallino, D. L. (1989). "The high risk occupational disease notification and prevention act: A good proposal that should be enacted into law. *Northern Kentucky Law Review* 17 (Fall): 119–133.

National Small Business United. (1993). "President's health care plan draws mixed response from small business owners." Press release, September 21.

Priest, D. (1994). "Pulse of health care reform debate likely to quicken." *Washington Post* (July 15): A4.

Rich, S., and A. Devroy (1994). "Chamber of Commerce opposes Clinton health plan." *Washington Post* (February 4): A12.

Schwartz, V. E. (1989). "Warning: occupational disease notification can be a liability nightmare." *Northern Kentucky Law Review* 17 (Fall): 105–117.

Seelye, K. Q. (1994). "The fall and amazing rise of Senator Bob Packwood." *New York Times* (July 10): E3.

Weisskopf, M. (1994a). "Health care lobbies lobby each other." *Washington Post* (March 1): A8.

———. (1994b). "Lobbyists shift into reverse." *Washington Post*. May 13: A3.

Case Studies: Social Security, Plant Shut-downs, and Striker Replacements

SOCIAL SECURITY

The major business lobbies have generally been opposed to the expansion of social security. The National Association of Manufacturers and Chamber of Commerce denounced social security when it was proposed during the 1930s as totalitarian. They now favor substantial privatization of the system. The justification that they and other critics provide is that the retiring baby boomers will bankrupt the system. However, this is merely pretext for continued opposition to a social program that demonstrates the potential of government activism.

In his essay, "A Radical Departure: Social Welfare and the Election," Ira Katznelson (1981) provides an explanation for the political resiliency of social security. He bases his analysis partly on the concept of the "social democratic minimum." The social democratic minimum is whatever measure of government intervention in the economy appears consistent with a broad and persisting consensus. Katznelson attributes this minimum to the need for economic intervention by the state merely to ensure the process of capital accumulation, and to guarantee social acceptance of this process. In other words, the social democratic minimum consists of a great compromise between capitalism and democracy, preserving capitalism in a modified form.

According to Katznelson:

The minimum varies from state to state and from time to time because it represents an amalgam of what has come to be economically, politically, and culturally necessary. The minimum is in part genuinely a minimum by intention that connotes widely shared meanings and understandings about the appropriate dimensions and character of government interventions in the market. Although largely the result of past group and class struggles, the minimum at a given moment is no longer the subject of struggle. It is accepted as a given by all classes in society. The existence of a National Health Service in Great Britain and a social security system in the United States are cases in point. (Katznelson 1981, p. 318)

Conservatives in the business lobbies have long been frustrated by frequent expansions of social security. They have never been part of the political consensus that Katznelson argues has sheltered the program. Now, apparently, business lobbies and investment fund managers perceive an opportunity to cut social security benefits and require senior citizens to rely more on private savings. Campaigns to roll back social insurance programs have gathered force throughout the developed world.

The major business lobbies want to persuade the public that social security is an unsound system. This argument is based on the notion that a social contract between citizens and their government requiring the pooling of resources to assure economic security for all is inherently unsustainable, since it socializes risk in the pursuit of greater equality. The alternative is "individual responsibility," however illusory this is in an economy dominated by large corporations that shield their investors from liability.

Why is it significant that the business lobbies favor privatization? Certainly many businesses have benefited by the sales underwritten by retirees' and others' social security benefits. This reality has convinced Katznelson that business leaders know not to challenge social security. However, ideology apparently trumps understanding. Social security is a successful program that legitimizes an activist state and reveals weaknesses in free market thinking. For these reasons, it is a threat to business lobby ideologues.

The NAM position on social security is reprinted below. Note that there is no compromise with the principle of social insurance in the NAM statement. NAM proposes nothing less than the disestablishment of the social security system.

WARREN L. BATTS

Chairman and CEO Tupperware Corporation and Chairman Premark International, Inc., on behalf of the National Association of Manufacturers before the Subcommittee on Social Security of the Ways and Means Committee, U.S. House of Representatives, on "The Future of Social Security," July 10, 1997 (NAM 1997).

Chairman Bunning, I am Warren Batts, Chairman and CEO of the Tupperware Corporation, and Chairman of Premark International, Inc., and of the National Association of Manufacturers. I am pleased to represent the NAM today in testifying before this subcommittee. . . .

Mr. Chairman, two programs of the federal government present significant threats to the continued vitality of the U.S. economy: One is Medicare; the other is the Social Security retirement system.

I don't make this statement for the sake of dramatic effect. In fact, if my objective were to shock the Subcommittee and members of the Congress, I could find words more pointed than that the programs "significantly threaten the vitality" of our national economy. The truth of the matter is that Medicare and Social Security constitute promises which are beyond the ability of the government to pay. The projected costs of the programs exceed the funds that will be available. And if government sought to raise enough additional funds through new levels of taxes necessary to pay for the continuing shortfall, the economy would simply get turned on its head, with both individuals and businesses contributing increasing portions of their earnings to pay for entitlement programs out of control.

Neither this economy nor any economy has the strength and resiliency to absorb the necessary level of tax increases to pay for these programs and remain competitive in the global marketplace. Global competition destroys those who are complacent or inefficient, or those whose organizing principles come from obsolete ideologies. If we lose our ability to compete effectively in this marketplace, our economy becomes static. At the very least, it can no longer grow; in fact, it is far more likely to decline.

And growth, Mr. Chairman, is what America is all about. America is an idea based on growth, where successive generations have invested their energy and human capital, no less than their savings, in hopes of material and social progress. And through economic growth America has achieved a high degree of fairness for individuals. Indeed, any lack of growth by specific groups within our American society is taken as an immediate signal of a lack of fairness.

As this century draws to a close, the rest of the world looks to us, even if it sometimes fails to admit it, and seems finally to have learned what Americans have known since the nation was founded: Economic growth is the best way of accomplishing· fairness for individuals within a society. Nations have burned their ideological textbooks, and are studying American institutions, beginning with the economic institution that is the individual.

Growth is achieved through investment of human and fiscal capital in productive enterprise. Such investment will continue only if the government forebears confiscating the savings of individuals and businesses in order to pay the compounding liabilities of unreformed entitlement programs.

Entitlement programs threaten our economic well-being collectively, and threaten the fairness to all of us as individuals. . . .

Economic growth through increased productivity and competitiveness of U.S. manufacturers remains the most significant goal pursued by the National Association of Manufacturers since its founding over 100 years ago. The significant attention by the NAM to the critical need to reform our entitlement programs indicates the relative importance we accord the issue. Even more than issues affecting trade, regulatory reform, or tax policy, the NAM has identified reform of the entitlement programs as the issue most important to economic growth for American business and economic independence for individuals. . . .

Reform or restructuring of the Medicare system is, of course, an enormous issue. In recent weeks, the Congress and the White House have shown increased awareness of the need to address Medicare more broadly. This series of hearings on the Social Security system provides evidence of increased debate of the issue. The title of these hearings, "The Future of Social Security," itself underscores growing popular awareness that the future of the Social Security system actually is in doubt. The NAM regards such doubts as well taken.

For over a decade, the NAM has warned of structural imbalance within the Social Security system and the necessity of fundamental reform. NAM attention to the issue quickened during 1995 and 1996, as popular perception of demographic changes affecting the system sharpened, and as the first legislative proposals appeared.

At its September 1996 meeting, the NAM Board approved a resolution on Social Security reform. In April of this year, the Board approved a "Statement of Principles" outlining its position on reform in greater detail. The Principles emphasize fairness for individuals and growth for the U.S. economy. . . .

While not endorsing any specific reform proposal yet put forward by legislators or public policy institutions, the NAM Principles address prerequisites to fundamental reform—features which a reformed system must possess in order to achieve the goals of fairness for individuals and growth for the U.S. economy.

Less obviously, but no less importantly, the Principles address the fact that structural imbalance of the current Social Security system, not merely insufficient funding, makes reform necessary. A fundamental distinction in testimony that this Subcommittee is likely to hear is between those who view "The Future of Social Security" as a funding issue, and those who see reform as a means of addressing structural imbalance of the current system. Count the NAM among the latter. . . .

In addressing structural imbalance of the current system, the first principle for reform is that savings for retirement be separated from the "safety net" of protection against poverty in old age.

Mr. Chairman and members of the Subcommittee, I probably don't have to tell you that what I've referred to as the "first principle"—that of segregating savings from social insurance—is the most controversial part of the debate over reform of the Social Security system.

From the point of view of those advocating reform, a separation of the savings function from the social insurance element of the current system is overwhelmingly obvious. Any business-person immediately recognizes that accumulation of reserves—"savings"—is a function entirely separate from protecting those reserves through the medium of insurance. Thus, the reaction of pragmatists, such as NAM members, is to make a separate savings function the first principle and cornerstone of reform.

I recognize, of course, that defenders of the current system are likely to disagree vehemently with my assertion that a decoupling of savings from safety-net is "obvious." If I understand their position, it is that the Social Security retirement system represents the great achievement of Twentieth Century liberal democracy—an intergenerational social compact for centralized and scheduled redistribution of funds acquired through federal taxing authority.

While I respect the right to such views, I disagree profoundly with the assumptions about individuals and about economics on which those views are based. But to spare this Subcommittee a discussion of political theory, I'll simply note that changing demographics are making the current system economically obsolete and unsustainable. Hence, our first principle for reform is that the social insurance element of "Social Security" be separated from the accumulation of retirement savings. . . .

The second NAM Principle is that individuals should have an ownership interest in the savings that they accumulate over their working lives. Individual ownership of retirement savings is not only obvious, but well established as a legal principle under pension law. Individuals retain a vested right to their accumulated retirement savings, protected by federal law. Further, such savings are to be accumulated until retirement, and not used for other purposes. In the event of an individual's premature death, the accumulated savings are available to their survivors and heirs.

In short, individuals should "own" their retirement savings, no less than they own a piece of real estate or shares of stock. . . .

The third NAM Principle for reform is that amounts saved by individuals for retirement should be held "for the exclusive benefit" of the person doing the savings. To this effect, the government itself should defer to pension law already on the books. The so-called "Exclusive Benefit" rule under ERISA means that retirement savings exist for one purpose—to provide income to an individual in retirement. Such savings exist for the singular purpose of providing retirement income for the individual who has saved the money. The government should have no right to control investment of the funds.

Accordingly, individuals' savings would be held in trust by fiduciaries responsible to the individuals who had saved the money. And within standards similar to those of ERISA, the individual would direct prudent investments. Obviously, this isn't to say that there would be no pooling of individual accounts—of course investment managers would pool accounts, in just the same way that hundreds of billions of dollars in pension plan investments and 401(k) plans are currently pooled. . . .

In addition, the NAM reform Principles emphasize the importance of implementing reforms as soon as possible. We all recognize the enormity of the transition funding issue. And while detailed proposals for an equitable means of transition funding await the development of econometric models, one thing remains overwhelmingly clear: Any solution to the issue of transition-period funding ultimately turns upon early implementation of reforms, so that the greatest number of individuals have the greatest amount of time to accumulate individual retirement savings, and thus, become less dependent upon the current Social Security system. . . .

PLANT SHUT-DOWNS AND STRIKER REPLACEMENTS

Most of my case studies provide evidence of business lobbies' unwillingness to compromise with labor and other stakeholders. The modest labor law reform bill debated in Congress in 1978, which would have accelerated National Labor Relations Board procedures and improved remedies for management unfair labor practices, was defeated by a filibuster which permitted practical conservatives (and their allies within the business lobbies) to frustrate the Senate majority. Labor leaders were outraged that unionized employers within the Business Roundtable were unable to secure Roundtable neutrality. (UAW President Douglas Fraser resigned from Dunlop's Labor-Management Group in protest of employer obstructionism on this issue as well as others) (Townley 1986).

In 1988, despite business opposition, Congress approved a measure requiring employers to provide at least ninety days notice of major lay-offs. President Reagan initially vetoed the bill but later allowed it to pass without his signature. One explanation for business rigidity with regard to such legislation is the fear of the "opening wedge." Malcolm Lovell, the chair of a commission on worker adjustment during the Reagan administration, argued that employers on the commission refused to consider labor's proposals for policies assisting workers on their merits, regarding any concession as equivalent to defeat.

Lovell explained:

- A further obstacle to a satisfactory resolution of the plant closing issue is a perception by some (although not all) business lobbyists that passage of any current labor-supported measure presages approval of a whole array of social legislation including parental leave, double-breasting in construction, risk notification, and minimum wage provisions. . . . Any approach which automatically assumes that which is proposed by the other side is intrinsically bad represents cynicism at its worst. (1987, p. 104)

Some of the recommendations of Lovell's commission with respect to public programs for worker adjustment met with general support from the Business Roundtable, the NAM, and the AFL-CIO. However, the Reagan administration and business interests favored voluntary advance notice, perhaps with tax incentives, rather than any form of mandated notice. Early versions of the plant closing legislation required employer consultation with workers prior to plant closings. Business lobbyists feared that even the most limited mandate would render increased regulation more likely in the future (Lovell 1987).

In its annual reports, the Committee for Economic Development has celebrated its success in blocking rigorous plant closing regulation. While business criticism resulted in substantial weakening of the plant closing legislation (the period of required notice was shortened and exceptions to the requirement were specified), organized business remained in opposition. The bill ultimately passed Congress because members of Congress were unpersuaded by the business lobbies' warnings of economic calamity.

The defeat of a bill to prohibit permanent replacement of striking workers by filibuster in July of 1994 underscores both the unwillingness of most Republicans and business lobbies to compromise on labor and social legislation and the centrality of the filibuster to conservative strategy. When asked what might soften his opposition to the measure, Republican leader Robert Dole (Kansas) suggested only that the Democrats withdraw it. Chamber of Commerce representatives said that "business regards this as a no-compromise issue." The National Association of Manufacturers applauded the success of the filibuster (*Baltimore Sun* 1994).

REFERENCES

Baltimore Sun. (1994). "Ban on replacing strikers facing doom in Senate." *Baltimore Sun* (July 13): 1A.

Katznelson, I. (1981). "A radical departure: Social welfare and the election." In T. Ferguson and J. Roger (eds.), *The hidden election: Politics and economics in the 1980 presidential campaign*. New York: Pantheon, pp. 313–340.

Lovell, M. (1987). "The task force on economic adjustment and worker displacement—A year later." *Proceedings of the fortieth annual meeting of the Industrial Relations Research Association*. Chicago: IRRA, pp. 100–106.

National Association of Manufacturers (1997). "NAM statement on social security." Http://www.nam.org.

Townley, B. (1986). *Labor law reform in U.S. industrial relations*. Brookfield, Vt.: Gower.

Civil Rights Act of 1991: An Exceptional Case

The behavior of the Business Roundtable with respect to the Civil Rights Act of 1991 represents an exception to business lobbies' tendency to oppose social legislation. On this issue, some major corporations appear to have been committed to the protection of the affirmative action plans that they had worked so hard to establish. The civil rights community wanted to amend the law to reinstate the *Griggs* doctrine (which empowered workers to challenge selection procedures that disproportionately excluded minority group members according to the notion of disparate impact) and otherwise undo the effects of conservative decisions of the Reagan/Bush Supreme Court. The Leadership Conference on Civil Rights and Business Roundtable entered into negotiations over the substance of a new civil rights bill until pressure from the Bush administration led to business withdrawal. (White House Chief of Staff John Sununu instructed AT&T executive Robert Allen to cease the negotiations in 1990 and 1991. However, after David Duke demonstrated considerable support in a Republican primary in Louisiana, President Bush thought it best to distance himself from Duke by abandoning his opposition to the Civil Rights Act.) (See Gould [1993, pp. 235–257].)

AT&T's involvement in the campaign to enact a new civil rights bill overturning adverse Supreme Court rulings is not surprising. The firm has profoundly restructured human resource practices in order to comply with consent decrees with the Equal Employment Opportunity Commission (EEOC) and Office of Federal Contract Compliance Programs. Prior to the landmark 1973 consent decree with both agencies, women had been relegated to jobs as operators and denied the opportunity to work in "outside" crafts and in management. African-Americans and Hispanics were poorly represented within the better-paying craft positions. The decree set goals and timetables for increased representation of women and minority group members within craft and managerial positions and established other programs to enhance equity at the enterprise. When the decree expired in 1979, AT&T introduced a voluntary affirmative action program.

AT&T management clearly came to perceive advantages in its affirmative action commitments. Given that AT&T has long been subject to extensive regulation by the Federal Communications Commission and state agencies, its leaders have recognized the value of maintaining good relations with stakeholder groups whose attitudes might affect the course of regulation. AT&T also is relatively highly unionized. The firm's experience with regulation and union contracts has accustomed it to compromise with stakeholders. AT&T's long-term investment in affirmative action may account for its efforts to undo the erosion of civil rights law in the 1980s[1] (see Gould [1993]).

Those Roundtable members who favored the negotiations with the Leadership Council on Civil Rights were potentially at odds with members who supported the Equal Employment Advisory Council (EEAC). The EEAC shares offices with the Labor Policy Association (and its association with the law firm of McGuiness and Williams) and generally seeks to relieve companies of many of the burdens of civil rights enforcement. AT&T contributes to the EEAC despite the latter's ultraconservative ideology.

There are, of course, AT&T executives who are unhappy with the firm's activities in defense of affirmative action. Their perspectives are evident in Herbert Northrup's volume on the consequences of the 1972 EEOC-AT&T consent decree. Throughout this book there are managers who warn that unqualified women and minority group members are being promoted as a result of the consent decree. Managers with these views provide the constituency for the Equal Employment Advisory Council, which is closely linked to the Labor Policy Association.

The Chamber of Commerce opposed negotiations with the Leadership Council (and opposed the Civil Rights Act of 1964 as well). The Chamber was prepared to support a rollback of affirmative action programs. This is now the position of a substantial number of Congressional Republicans. Affirmative action clearly divides the business community; it is one issue on which the Business Roundtable leaves the ideological company of other business lobbies.

NOTE

1. Executives may realize that complying with affirmative action goals and timetables is preferable to one alternative approach to assuring equal opportunity: government scrutiny of each employment decision.

REFERENCES

Gould, W. L. (1993). *Agenda for reform: The future of employment relationships and the law*. Cambridge, Mass: MIT Press.

Northrup, H. R., and J. Larson. (1981). *The impact of the AT&T-EEO consent decree*. Philadelphia: Industrial Research Unit, Wharton School, University of Pennsylvania.

Pressures on the Business Lobbies: Dominant Minorities and Internationalization

DOMINANT MINORITIES

Mainstream business associations are predisposed to lean significantly to the right because they are united by a commitment to the defense of managerial interests. An active minority of their mostly passive members interprets this commitment to require opposition to any government initiatives that limit managerial discretion. Both the National Association of Manufacturers and the Chamber of Commerce are especially sensitive to small groups of big businesses. Economist Mancur Olson was one of many scholars who have noted this. He writes, "A number of very large businesses will gain or lose so much from changes in national policy that they will find it expedient to make significant contributions." Olson says that the NAM is "in practice supported and controlled by a handful of really big businesses" (Olson 1965, pp. 146–147). Levitan and Cooper (1984, p. 19) stress the preponderance of executives from large enterprises on the NAM and Chamber governing boards.

The small groups of big businesses that dominate the Chamber and NAM are usually extremely conservative. These businesses' access to the Republican party provides them with another avenue to influence the course of the lobbies. Journalist Michael Lind (1996, p. 81) suggests yet another factor reinforcing lobby conservatism. William Simon, treasury secretary under Nixon and Ford, became president of the John M. Olin Foundation in 1976 and led a renewed effort to shape public opinion in alliance with a few other business-oriented foundations. Simon aimed to combat what he perceived as a "dominant socialist-statist-collectivist orthodoxy which prevails in much of the media, in most of our large universities, among many of our politicians, and tragically, among not a few of our top business executives." Olin Corporation and Olin Foundation funds have been available to reward think tanks and business lobbies for hewing to a strictly conservative line.

Business in the non-union south and west provides a fertile constituency for business lobby conservatism. The conservative politics of southern and western states reflect a business-dominated political economy with weak labor and other social movements. The current House Republican majority is led by not a few right-wing businessmen-turned-politicians from the south (for example, Cass Ballenger of North Carolina, industrialist and longtime foe of the Occupational Safety and Health Administration).

OLIGARCHY AND ARISTOCRACY

Political philosophers have long explored the virtues of mixed forms of government. The writers of *The Federalist Papers* called for a republican form of government that would have aristocratic qualities in that representatives of the people would be more qualified to govern than the people themselves. The Senate was conceived as an organ for the representation of an elite, and the House was to be the more "democratic" element of government. The Presidency reflected the principle of monarchy. The Federalists admired the inherent "balance" of the "English Constitution," in which monarchy, aristocracy (the House of Lords), and democracy (the House of Commons) were assigned roles.

Thomas Jefferson, John Adams, and Alexander Hamilton all professed devotion to republican principles. They agreed that popular participation should play a role in government. They disagreed as the proper proportions of elite and popular rule. Jefferson favored a "democratic republic" in which an educated citizenry would govern themselves through representatives. Adams preferred a political system that would balance elite rule with a measure of democracy. Hamilton desired a government that would use a pinch of democracy to stabilize and perfect, rather than restrain, elite rule.

The U.S. political system remains a mixed form. While the Senate no longer is explicitly the aristocratic component, the federal political structure has many features that provide political benefits to economic elites. The enduring issue of states' rights has served as a shield for elites to maintain their political power. Initially, the slave owners claimed the mantle of states' rights in order to protect the system of slavery. Following the abolition of slavery, the Bourbons fought to maintain a low wage regime including sharecropping and other exploitive practices. New Deal labor law was written in such a way as to leave these practices nearly untouched. Agricultural and domestic workers have historically lacked coverage under labor law. The southern conservatives have had the power in the Senate through the filibuster and committee chairmanships to influence national politics. They have sought to protect an oligarchic sub-system in American politics.

In *Up from Conservatism: Why the Right Is Wrong for America,* Michael Lind (1996) writes of the southernization of American politics. By this he means the increasing power of southern conservatives in the Republican party. No longer Dixiecrat Democrats, these Southern Republicans are seeking to rollback civil rights legislation and lift the burden of other regulation from business. They would like to extend the historic Southern model of one-party politics and undiluted management authority nationally. Business leaders in the Chamber of Commerce and NAM support this effort.

Lind explains:

The southernization of the right . . . means the adoption, by the leaders and intellectuals of the American right, of a "culture-war" approach to politics that was perfected by southern conservative Democrats during the period of their one-party rule in the South. . . . It means, as well, the adoption by the Republican leadership of a "southern" rather than a "northern" vision of the future of American capitalism and American politics—a vision of the United States as a low-wage, low-tax, low-investment industrial society like the New South of 1875–1965, a kind of early twentieth-century Mississippi or Alabama recreated on a continental scale. (1996, pp. 123–124)

The southern component in this process can be overstated. The mixed form of government in the United States has allowed local elites throughout the nation to consolidate their power. One-party, pro-business politics exists in rural areas and cities outside of the south. Only in particular regions and particular states have labor and other stakeholder groups acquired sufficient power to fundamentally democratize politics. (For example, the hostility of many conservatives to New York City reflects their distaste for the power labor and minority group members have often exercised there.)

Business leaders in the Chamber and allied organizations do not admit that they favor oligarchical politics with a superficial layer of democracy. Curiously, the concept of "business climate" is closely associated with the political system many business conservatives desire. Chamber leaders consider unionization, environmental regulation, health and safety standards, product liability lawsuits, and the like to threaten the business climate. In other words, states with powerful labor and environmental movements and pluralistic politics have a poor business climate.

INTERNATIONALIZATION

The apparent decline of sophisticated conservatism within the business community and the rightward drift of even such organizations as the Committee for Economic Development may result in part from the internationalization of the economy. Sociologist Richard Flacks writes:

In the '60s, Kennedy and Johnson were able to persuade significant numbers of big-business leaders to support or acquiesce to reform in order to sustain economic growth and dampen social unrest. . . .[Today] it appears that, in the global economy, corporate elites no longer care very much about American domestic society and, therefore, have no particular will to overcome the political and ideological resistance . . . to the welfare state. (1996, p. 4)[1]

It is likely that intensified competition with low-wage enterprises abroad stimulates a cost-consciousness among American employers and increases resistance to the burdens of social legislation. This in turn reduces the likelihood of deviations in the hard-line conservatism of business lobbies.

. The enactment of the North American Free Trade Agreement and of its proposed extension is likely to reinforce business hostility to social legislation. NAFTA permits U.S. firms to escape social regulation in the United

States by investing in Mexico. Just as the southern political economy has functioned as a brake on social legislation in the United States the option of Mexican investment diminishes the prospects for compromise between business and other stakeholder groups.

U.S. business lobbies have alliances with business associations throughout the world. The result is an international chorus for deregulation. In the developed nations of the West, there is considerable anxiety about internationalization, and the parties of the left have so far provided few clear and credible alternatives to business calls for deregulation and budget cuts. The Fraser Institute in Canada and the New Zealand Business Roundtable are among those business groups preaching market reform. Their success in swaying governments allows their allies to argue that free markets reforms are sweeping the world.

On the other hand, in some cases, internationalization may have rather different consequences for business politics. If local business interests perceive a threat in internationalization, they may be prepared to cooperate with labor and other groups in the development of a program that sustains the local economy. This would not result in a dogmatic opposition to social legislation. In Quebec, a segment of local business has chosen not to fight pro-labor legislation banning on the hiring of replacement workers during strikes and requiring the extension of union wage levels throughout an industry in a concession to the politics of separatism.

NOTE

1. The reader need not share Flacks' left-wing politics to agree that international competition might reduce business acceptance of the domestic welfare state. Note that *Keeping America Competitive* from the Employment Policy Foundation,

excerpted in chapter three, suggests that the domestic regulation of labor standards renders U.S. firms uncompetitive.

REFERENCES

Flacks, R. (1996). "Taking ideology seriously: a route to progressive power." Http://www.socialpolicy.org/95winter/flacks.html.

Levitan, S. A., and M. Cooper. (1984). *Business lobbies: The public good and the bottom line*. Baltimore: Johns Hopkins University Press.

Lind, M. (1996). *Up from conservatism: Why the right is wrong for America*. New York: The Free Press.

Olson, M. (1965). *The logic of collective action*. Cambridge, Mass.: Harvard University Press.

CHAPTER EIGHT

Business Liberalism

Edward Filene, the founder of Filene's Department Store and the Twentieth Century Fund (now the Century Foundation), wrote:

I do not know of a better word [other than liberal] for describing the sort of business man who broadly speaking, is the opposite of the reactionary, the sort of business man who faces fresh problems with a fresh mind, who is more interested in creating a better order of things than in defending the existing order of things, who realizes that a private business is a public trust, and who has a greater reverence for scientific method than for the traditions and majority opinion of his class.

Filene, who died in 1937, did in fact endure much criticism from fellow business executives for his surrender of power within his store to councils of workers and his warm embrace of the New Deal. In his mind, the business enterprise is a social contract among workers, managers, consumers, community, and government, and the quality of this contract is determined by the justice and integrity of the underlying bargains (1924, pp. 284–285).

Filene was a founder of the Chamber of Commerce but came to view this organization as a troubling symbol of the reactionary politics of the business community. He resigned in the 1930s.

It is likely that Filene's liberalism was the result of the values he brought to his work rather than a consequence of his business experience. However, he claimed that his liberalism derived from a scientific examination of business problems, and that, in particular, the potential of mass production required profound reform of business. Like Henry Ford, although more sincerely than Ford, Filene believed that workers should earn sufficient income to purchase the products of their labor. Thus, he argued, business leaders should be enthusiastic advocates of pay increases. In order to sustain purchasing power and relieve debt, Filene promoted credit unions as an alternative to traditional banks. He experimented with industrial democracy in his own enterprise, Filene's Department Store, and looked favorably upon the labor movement. His progressive experimentation led to his being ousted from management at Filene's, leaving him with substantial income but no business. (Filene then founded the Twentieth Century Fund to promote the cause of reform in business and politics.)

FILENE'S OWN WORDS

This 1924 essay by Edward Filene very clearly identified the forces inhibiting progressive ideas within the business community. Note that he described the dogmatic conservatism of business associations and attributed it to the superior wealth and organization of the right-wing constituency and to the absence of significant social contact between business leaders and other social groups, among other factors (Filene 1924, pp. 284–306).

THE LIBERAL BUSINESS MAN
UNDER FIRE

I

ON ALMOST every page of this book I have emphasized, directly or by implication, the importance of business liberalism in business leadership. I dislike to use the word "liberalism" in this connection. It is a rather battered and weather-beaten word; it has come to have, in many minds, all sorts of implications that one would never associate with effective business leadership; it has been captured by the armchair strategists and irresponsible doctrinaires; it has become the storm center of a motley array of antagonisms and prejudices. But it is, after all, a good word with worthy traditions. That it has now and then fallen into bad company is no justification for throwing it away.

I do not know of a better word for describing the sort of business man who, broadly speaking, is the opposite of the reactionary, the sort of business man who faces fresh problems with a fresh mind, who is more interested in creating a better order of things than in defending the existing order of things, who realizes that a private business is a public trust, and who has greater reverence for scientific method than for the traditions and majority opinion of his class. It is this sort of business man who will, as I see it, be best able to meet the challenge of the difficult time ahead; it is this sort of business man who will make the big business successes of the next ten or twenty years.

But, strange to say, despite the fact that liberal business policies will underlie large business success, the liberal business man will find that he will have to pay a very definite price for his liberalism. The business man who insists upon approaching the problems of business and industry in a scientific and liberal spirit sooner or later brings down upon his head the criticism of important groups of his fellow business men. There is no use discounting the fact that the liberal business man is still a somewhat lonely figure in the councils of American business and industrial leadership. Invariably a few ultraconservative business men wage a propaganda war against the business man who attempts to accelerate the pace of progress, especially if he attempts to speed up that democratization of industry upon which social peace and efficiency must increasingly depend.

This opposition is the last thing we should expect from men whose material success, one would suppose, depends upon their being as ready to scrap an outworn idea as to discard an outworn machine. But the fact remains! And this "loneliness of the liberal" in business circles is a thing that must come in for careful consideration in any comprehensive study of the factors that will make for the arrest or advancement of both successful business and social progress during the next ten or twenty years.

The attitude which the average business man takes toward one of his fellows who represents the sort of liberalism that comes from a scientific study of business and social problems would furnish the clue for an interesting study. I wish that some one of our distinguished psychologists would give us a realistic study of how successful business men think and act. Such a study would, of course, have to begin with an examination of how successful business men think and act inside their own businesses, but this examination would be only the starting point for a much-needed study of how successful business men think and act when they work in the committees or control the policies of local, state, and national organizations dealing with issues of large social significance.

If the business men who were the subjects of such a study had conceived business in a broadly scientific way, it would be found that the qualities that had made them successful in business were the very qualities that would make them a creative and liberalizing influence in organizations dealing with matters of wide social concern to city, state, and nation. But I fear that such a study would reveal the fact that, in many instances, business success had been interpreted so thoroughly in terms of immediate profits that the qualities of mind which had brought the conventional success to the business men were qualities that later interfered with their public service.

We should expect that the man who had been successful in business would bring the spirit of the impartial investigator, the inventor, the innovator, the pioneer to any issue in any field. By all the laws of logic, the men who have been most successful in business should be the most progressive in matters outside their business. In the years of change and challenge that lie just ahead of us I think this will be true, but to date the contrary has been true in a distressingly large number of instances. Certainly I cannot be accused of treason to my class for setting down the obvious fact that many conspicuously successful business men display an astounding lack of vision in the larger matters of social and industrial policy that lie outside their immediate businesses.

II

But it is not the merely negative conservatism of certain successful business men that I have in mind just now. I am thinking of the successful business men who take their conservatism very seriously when they serve upon the directorates of local, state, and national organizations of business men and other social groups. . . . Over and over again, in organizations of business men, I have seen groups of entirely honest and eminently successful men turn against and label as dangerous one of their fellows who was only reasonably progressive. I have seen such men display an utter inability to distinguish between sane social advance and revolutionary socialism. I think that one of the books we business men should keep always on our desks is a book of synonyms. It might help us to avoid branding straight thinking as radicalism.

I have seen groups of highly successful business men honestly oppose the most obviously elementary steps toward conservative social betterment. For instance, it is obvious that the only hope of arriving at a constructive programme of industrial relations is through cooperation, through the getting together of the leaders of the employing group and leaders of the employed group. It is in the council chamber, not on the battlefield, that we shall resolve the conflicts of industry. Industrial peace will not come as the by-product of a fight, but as the result of industrial statesmanship. This is the veriest primer logic. And yet the leaders of many of our national organizations of business men have steadfastly refused to sit down in conference with the leaders of organized labor.

The business men in these organizations who have insisted upon such a rapprochement have been in the minority. And by their insistence upon this essentially conservative and business-like procedure they have succeeded only in courting the suspicion of their associates. They have been rewarded for their pains with a reputation for radicalism that hampers them for further influence in business circles.

The conservative business man apparently does not realize that if he were wholly successful in his opposition to his more liberal associate there would be left no method of progress except revolution. As it is, his partially successful opposition slows down progress unnecessarily. If my contention—that the social progress of the future will be achieved through the development rather than the destruction of the business system—is sound, we must somehow succeed in reducing if not removing this opposition to the liberal business man which to-day characterizes the policy of so many business men's organizations.

III

As a first step we must make a real study of the motives and technics of both the conservative and the liberal business man. Maybe both are to blame for this socially dangerous schism in business councils. This chapter does not, in any sense, pretend to be the basic study we need. I want only to put down a few conclusions that I have reached as a result of a good many years spent in the inner councils of business and in local, national, and international organizations of business men dealing with those larger policies of business and industry which root in and react upon social and political conditions. It may be that these conclusions will prompt someone to make the exhaustive study of the business mind which is greatly needed.

Now, it is the easiest thing in the world to write a fervent indictment of the static, tradition-bound, conservative mind. Hardly a week passes without an emotional broadside fired from some quarter at the conservative. Even if I were inclined to do it, it would be wasteful duplication for me to repeat this performance. Probably the most important study of the conservative mind that has been made in the present generation is to be found in James Harvey Robinson's "The Mind in the Making." It is not the arm-chair-and-carpet-slippers sort of book that our scholars too often give us. It is an intensely practical book. It explains to the conservative why he is conservative. And it is this sort of explanation rather than emotional denunciation that will help us to clear up the misunderstanding that lies back of the opposition that the liberal business man encounters among his associates. We business men, if we are to survive and succeed in the future, will have to take to heart Mr. Robinson's appeal for the creation of "an unprecedented condition and to utilize unprecedented knowledge." But, as I have said, I am not undertaking here the basic study which I suggest as urgently needed. I want, however, to make two observations about the fact and effectiveness of the conservatism of successful business men.

One of the reasons, I am sure, why many successful business men are predisposed to a conservative if not reactionary point of view is that they do not, as a rule, have enough social and recreational contacts with men of other classes, other interests, and other points of view. Even inside his business, the average business man trains pretty consistently with his own crowd, that is, with the administrative, the controlling, the directing group. He maintains too rigidly the conventional relation of the "boss" to the other groups in his business. And outside office hours, the average business man is too much given to spending his time in the hunting lodge, on the golf links, or in the metropolitan club, where, taken by and large, he meets only the men who share his point of view. This means that the average business man is carefully insulated from that social contact, that give and take of discussion with men of different social rank, different race, and different points of view, which is so necessary in checking up, correcting, and humanizing one's outlook upon life and its issues. The mental point of view that results from training too much with one's own class accounts, I am sure, for the fact of much business conservatism.

And one of the reasons why conservative business men usually succeed in their opposition to their more liberal associates is because the cause of conservatism is invariably better organized than the cause of liberalism. In the average business men's organization, it will be found that the men who approach the problems of business and labor from the stock-market point of view excel their more liberal associates in the organization of a staff of secretaries, experts, and publicity men who help them dramatize and push their policy through the councils of the organization. These staffs of secretaries, experts, and publicity men are maintained as part of their business organizations by some of the abler conservative business men. These staffs not only function at the time of great national meetings but influence the public mind ad interim. The plain fact is that our conservative business men employ more machinery and more money for expressing and maintaining their point of view than our liberal business men employ and they regard such expenditure as legitimate business expense.

But I should like to bring this discussion down to the individual business man and away from problems of organization and expenditure. From a lifetime spent in dealing with both conservative and liberal business men inside and outside business I am able to see at least six reasons why the liberal business man faces such persistent opposition at the hands of his fellows. Let me state them simply, without unduly extending this chapter.

IV

First, it lies in the very nature of things that the man whose ideas are a little in advance of the ideas of his associates will sooner or later find himself opposed and, if possible, set aside. As men grow older they are likely to grow more conservative. By the time they have achieved success they are likely to have lost some of their eager appetite for adventure and experiment. The liberal in business insists upon continuing experimentation, but he is likely to find that the majority of his associates who were his enthusiastic helpers in the working out of his first ventures are content with the measure of their first great success and see no use in disturbing what is already a success by trying still other experiments. The story of the average business man's career is the story of a settling down, beginning with the willingness to experiment which resulted in his first success, and ending with a self-satisfied and routine administration of established methods. Now, it is inevitable that any business man who is always looking ahead for improved methods and broader policies is, by this very effort, going to make himself unpopular with the men who are satisfied with established things, especially if the established things are profitable.

This opposition to the liberal in business has nothing to do with the goodness or badness of his opponents. If his training has made him conservative, a "good" man is just as likely as a "bad" man to be the suspicious critic and determined opponent of the business man who aligns himself with new forces and new movements.

It is a problem in human nature that we are facing. As men grow older they are disposed to cling to the esteem and friendship of their fellows and shrink from any nonconformity that might jeopardize their reputations for good form in thought and action. As their youthful enthusiasms cool they have less and less desire to crusade for causes that will mature after they are dead, so they instinctively feel that their liberal associate and his ideas are to be discouraged, and as far as they can they rob him of any power to disturb them in their serenity and orderly procedure.

But when I speak of the liberal business man I am not thinking of the liberalism which has its roots only in youthful bravado, youthful willingness to take risks. That sort of liberalism, I suppose, cannot be expected of men as they grow older. I am thinking of a business liberalism that comes not from youthful enthusiasm but from straight thinking. I am thinking of the liberal business man who fights for progressive policies in business and in industry, not because they afford an opportunity for battle and adventure, but because they are essential to the permanently profitable future of business as well as to sound social advance. We can, perhaps, forgive the established business man for feeling a little irritation at the sometimes intolerant and dogmatic liberalism of inexperienced youth, but what is there in the liberalism of straight thinking that evokes such opposition? This leads me to the observations I want particularly to make. The opposition to the liberal business man is not due entirely to the conservatism of conservative men. It is due partly to personal and psychological reasons to be found in the liberal business man himself. The last five of the six reasons I set out to state have to do with these personal aspects of the problem.

V

Second, the liberal business man has arrived at his liberal conception of business policies because he thinks more scientifically than do his more conservative associates. He reasons more accurately from cause to effect. He succeeds more nearly than they in taking into account all the factors, human or material, that are involved in business administration. The scope and the scientific quality of his thinking enable him to anticipate conditions and to sense the policies that the business of the future will demand in a way that the average conservative and conventional business man does not and cannot. This means that, time and again, the liberal business man insists upon the urgent necessity of policies that his conservative associates have not yet visualized. His conclusion rests upon a hundred and one factors that the conventional business mind does not take into account. The up-shot of the matter is that very often a policy that seems the most elementary common sense to the liberal business man is looked upon as the erratic theorizing of an impractical idealism and calls out the opposition of his fellow. As someone has suggested, to see what is ignored by all is a fairly sure way to be ignored by all.

VI

Third, just because the liberal business man sees as imperative things that his conservative associates do not see at all, he often finds that his persistent fight for his policies is interpreted as obstinacy. They cannot understand his irritating insistence, in season and out of season, upon policies that seem to them, at best, only interesting theories. They are not mere theories to the liberal business man; they are inescapable deductions from facts that have been overlooked by the conservatives. He knows their importance to the business progress of the future, and a sense of obligation prompts him to wage an unceasing fight for their adoption. But what is, to him, a sense of obligation is interpreted by his associates as bullish obstinacy.

VII

Fourth, another thing that contributes to the unpopularity of the liberal in business is the normal impatience of the liberal mind. The very fact that a man has broken through the conservatism that a business career tends to induce implies a creative quality in his mind. And the man with a creative mind is likely to be impatient with the slower mental processes of his more conservative associates. If he does not keep constantly in mind the fact that the success of his policies is absolutely dependent upon the cooperation of his fellow business men, he is likely to betray his impatience in a manner that will hasten and intensify the opposition that his policies would normally stir up. If there is any man in the world upon whom the obligation of tolerance and diplomacy rests heavily it is the liberal in business—and there is no man for whom it is harder.

VIII

Fifth, the liberal business man is, in many instances, largely responsible for his own defeat because he is singularly open to the temptation to neglect the necessary advance work for his ideas among his associates. He is likely to overlook the necessity of undergoing the intolerable fatigue of persuasion. He is likely to thrust a new idea upon the attention of his associates with no previous explanation, and be ignored or outvoted because "safety first" is the rule that governs most people and because most of his associates are probably satisfied for the time with the success already achieved. As I have already said, the liberal business man is particularly susceptible to the two sins that he, of all men, should avoid—the sins of an intolerant spirit and an autocratic method. The liberal business man is likely to be intolerant because he cannot understand why the thing that has struck him instantly is not equally clear to the other fellow.

Now, the liberal business man must realize that he can work out his ideals only through human beings. He must realize that the first business of reform is to succeed. He is a democrat, and he must remember that the first law of democracy is that the leader agrees to go only as fast as he can carry his associates with him. It may be that truth crushed to earth will rise again, but it is the business of the liberal to see that truth is not crushed to earth in the first place. And this means that the liberal business man must be a patient teacher and good lobbyist. He cannot succeed by autocratic insistence upon his ideas.

IX

Sixth, the constant opposition that the liberal business man faces often forces him into an excessive concentration upon his ideals which makes him forget the normal courtesies and amenities of human relations, thereby confirming his opponents in their opposition. After all, there is no need and no excuse for sacrificing all of the things that make a man a congenial companion. You cannot imagine yourself getting chummy with Savonarola. I suppose the progress of the race depends upon the occasional ministry of the man who forgets the amiabilities of life in his fanatic concentration upon his ideals. But most of the wholesome and progressive work of the world must be done by the congenial cooperation of men who do not get on each other's nerves. The liberal business man must, therefore, avoid an excessive concentration upon his particular ideas that would make him an undesirable companion for conservatives, either on a fishing trip or in the committee room.

I do not want to seem to dismiss the subject of this chapter with a discussion of the art of being an agreeable dinner companion, but I do want to emphasize the fact that the liberal business man is obligated to see to it that his personality and his methods do not unnecessarily add to the normal opposition that liberalism always encounters. There are no general policies or adventures in organized effort that can solve this problem. It is a personal problem that the individual liberal in business must solve for himself.

X

I have, however, two suggestions regarding organized efforts that might clear the road of business and social progress a little. The first has to do with reducing the conservatism of the conservative; the second has to do with making the liberalism of the liberal a little more effective.

I said earlier in this chapter that one of the reasons why so many successful business men are predisposed to a conservative if not reactionary point of view is that they do not as a rule have enough social and recreational contacts with men of other classes, other interests, and other points of view. Now, I do not believe that the average business man is wholly to blame for his suicidal exclusiveness. As a people, we have given very little thought to devising ways and means for bringing all classes and all types of minds of our communities into contact. Men are not going to visit across the frontiers that separate social classes and divergent points of view unless special arrangements are made for such intercourse. It may be very narrowing, but birds of a feather do flock together. Now, I suggest that it would be invaluable if we could have in every community one club at least which aimed not at uniformity but at diversity in its membership, a club that afforded a common meeting ground for radical and conservative, for men of all social classes and of all races. Such club, a club that would be a club of clubs, with a mass membership and low dues, could be a sort of social and intellectual melting pot for the community. This is the principle that underlay the organization and accounts for the success of the City Club of Boston, which has a membership of about seven thousand. But that is another story for another time. I am concerned here only to suggest that we should provide machinery for the sort of social mixing that will reduce the extreme cocksureness of conservatives as well as the intolerance of the radical.

Again, I said earlier in this chapter that very often the conservative defeats the liberal because he employs better machinery and more money in support of his point of view. Now, I am aware of the sinister implications of propaganda by organized groups, but I submit that if the principles advanced effectively by conservative groups are too narrow to embrace the general public interest, they must, in the public interest, be opposed by liberal groups. If the liberal minority among business men are to counter the activity of their more numerous conservative associates, they must duplicate the machinery used by the conservative majority. To do this liberal business men must have equally effective staffs of secretaries, experts, and publicity men, and must have access to equally adequate funds. Unfortunately funds for the promotion of liberalism are difficult to obtain, for the general public does not see the need of such elaborate and carefully thought out effort as clearly as the liberal business man sees it. As a rule the public expects miracles to happen for the right. The liberal business man has learned from business experience that the right cannot depend simply upon its rightness for success. He knows that sound business and social progress can be achieved only by virtue of organized effort as carefully planned and as adequately financed as the organized effort of the conservative business groups. A clear recognition, then, that business liberalism must fight business conservatism upon its own ground and with its own methods is important.

The "loneliness of the liberal" in business circles must be carefully considered in any comprehensive study of the factors that will determine the arrest or the advancement of successful business and social progress during the next ten or twenty years.

BUSINESS FOR SOCIAL RESPONSIBILITY

Filene has had few peers in his liberal activism. The contemporary example of Business for Social Responsibility (BSR) illustrates the difficulties a reform-oriented business association has in establishing an alternative to the approach of mainstream business lobbies.

Many of the founders of BSR hoped that it would become an alternative to the Chamber of Commerce, lobbying on business issues from a more progressive perspective. BSR was launched by members of the Social Venture Network

(SVN), an exclusive, ideologically united group of business reformers. However, BSR has come to value growth over principle, inclusiveness at the expense of ideological coherence. The organization has responded with enthusiasm to the wishes of major corporate leaders (seeking public recognition for their initiatives in social responsibility) to join; this can only dilute the reformist commitments of the founders. BSR now de-emphasizes its role in Washington.

I interviewed Susan Spriggs, a BSR activist and Body Shop franchise-owner, at one of her stores.[1]

Susan Spriggs: We became the first American franchisees for the Body Shop and that was in 1990. There were four existing stores here. And all of us went into the business . . . it was our first time in retail. We were in other professions and my business partner, Marianne Mills, was doing public relations in New York City for the Body Shop and introduced us to the organization, introduced us to Anita [Roddick, chief executive of the Body Shop]. And we loved the concept. At that point it was the idea that you can mix business and service. All of us have a history of working in business and service. . . .

My history is a degree in urban studies. [I] worked for years in more urban-related and kind of race-related issues. I worked in equal opportunity employment for a long time. Marianne and Helen are, of course, sisters and have more environmental and kind of anti-nuke experience. And Helen had an insurance business, Marianne was in public relations and I was in management and recruiting. When we learned about the Body Shop, again, to repeat it, we loved the idea that we could bring our social concerns as well as our love for business to our job. So we second-mortgaged our homes, cleared out our 401ks, hocked our socks, left our jobs. Helen stayed with her insurance company and became a part of the franchise. And so, at that point in time, the business organizations that were available to us were organizations like the Chamber of Commerce. Helen became very quickly involved with the Social Venture Network. . . .

It is a group of individuals who formed an organization to work out societal issues. They're folks from academia and business and individuals who come together to talk about social concerns and to see what impact they can have on social concerns....

I think many people understood [that] the Social Venture Network fulfilled a very important need in their lives. And people from business were increasingly becoming part of the Social Venture Network. The idea was there.... Should there be a separate organization that dealt with business issues, business and social responsibility? And that's where the idea came from, it came from SVN....

[SVN] was founded by Chuck Blitz ... out of California and ... Josh Mailman. I think that Chuck Blitz and Josh founded SVN. ... I'm not a member of SVN....

Josh inherited ... has quite a bit of family money and he's done an amazing job of taking it and helping individuals in society and very concerned, always has been, about giving back and about these issues....

In 1992 a group of 53 businesses launched Business for Social Responsibility.... The membership has changed tremendously. Yes, I think a lot of these 53 people came from SVN so they had a common interest. Calvert Group, Body Shop, Ben and Jerry's. Anita Roddick, founder of the Body Shop, was on the front page of *USA Today* launching this new business organization. By 1994, Bill Clinton spoke at the ... annual conference, so it became, it moved from a fringe organization to much more of a mainstream organization.... Arnold Hiatt spoke [at the annual conference of BSR] and said that we can't have a healthy business in an unhealthy society. And so, we are here to say business has more responsibilities than just to make a profit....

I want to draw a contrast for you with the Chamber of Commerce.... Around the time that BSR was forming and people in SVN were going through these discussions of do we need a business organization ... we were being invited to join the Chamber. And there were two major accomplishments that the Chamber had had that year [in Fairfax County].... They had successfully held back the recycling bill.... That was a message to us. Business organizations that might represent us in other areas represent us [poorly on some of] those issues that are so strong for us. I guess in a way [that on specialized issues we differed] from the Chamber. . . . We're a member of the Arlington Chamber of Commerce and I would be a member of other Chambers if I had the time and the energy. There is a purpose that they serve. It just happens that they don't serve this special purpose that we are very interested in, and that is about business and social responsibility and giving back to the community. . . .

It became clear and obvious that if [BSR] were going to be including companies like Coca-Cola or any large corporation that they are not going to appreciate some of the things, lobbying on some of the issues that the smaller companies, liberal and left organizations were wanting [BSR] to lobby on. They made the decision to be inclusive to all companies, that the way that they could, they used the words "lead and learn" . . . companies could lead and learn in this area and join them and hear about good practices.

Here is the mission statement of BSR (1997).

BSR MISSION STATEMENT

Business for Social Responsibility is an alliance of businesses that defines, supports and promotes responsible business policies and practices that benefit not only our companies, but also our employees and communities, our economy and environment. BSR seeks to reshape the way business does business so that members and other companies can best address the many problems and opportunities that face both business and society.

BSR STATEMENT OF VALUES

The programs, activities and operating principles of Business for Social Responsibility are based on the following values and beliefs:

Prosperity and Well-Being

Responsible policies and practices enhance the commercial success of businesses, create a more hospitable climate for the conduct of business and enhance the well-being of people in communities where we conduct business and throughout the world.

Responsibility and Leadership

The impact and resources of business create responsibilities to our employees, customers, business partners, communities and the environment, as well as our shareholders.

Stewardship and Sustainability

Our businesses and society can best prosper when all citizens have access to quality education, health care, housing, a healthy and safe environment, and the opportunities created by our market economy; and when we promote sustainable development, peace and security for all citizens.

Diversity

We recognize, value and benefit from the diversity of our employees, neighbors and customers.

Partnership and Advocacy

Members of the business community should partner with one another and representatives of those impacted by business decisions to define, implement and promote policies and practices of responsible corporate citizenship.

Evolving Goals

Socially responsible corporate goals, policies, and practices are not static; companies need to continually review standards, needs, and concerns of their various stakeholders.

Universal Commitment

Responsible policies and practices should be implemented wherever businesses do business, in the United States and throughout the world.

BSR STATEMENT OF OPERATING PRINCIPLES

1. BSR will focus on policies and practices for the workplace, the marketplace, the environment and our communities at home and abroad that address the opportunities and concerns facing companies and the world in which we live.

2. BSR is an inclusive organization seeking to recruit, service and benefit companies that have already implemented or are committed to implementing significant socially responsible policies and practices as well as companies that are seeking to learn more about such policies and practices.

3. BSR is committed to an expanding membership through recruitment of large, medium and small size, and entrepreneurial companies.

4. BSR will develop a diverse membership and leadership.

5. BSR seeks specific, identifiable outcomes (e.g., products, actions and projects) when establishing priorities and initiatives.

6. BSR will seek the opinions and expertise of its members and partnerships with other private and public organizations (such as the BSR Education Fund) with which it shares interests and concerns.

7. BSR will operate consistent with the principles it advocates through its own workplace, environmental and local and global community policies and will act in an exemplary, ethical manner.

8. BSR will finance its core services and programs provided by its national and regional offices through the fees and contributions of its members and other businesses; it will develop relationships with foundations, public sector groups and individuals in order to finance special initiatives.

9. BSR is committed to the prudent management of the assets and resources of the organization.

10. We seek to embrace and employ leading edge and innovative technologies available to the organization.

NOTE

1. Interview with Susan Spriggs of Soapbox Trading/The Body Shop, Washington, D.C., August 15, 1997.

REFERENCES

Business for Social Responsibility. (1997). *BSR mission statement*. Http://www.bsr.org.

Filene, E. A. (1924). *The way out: A forecast of coming changes in American business and industry*. Garden City, N.Y.: Doubleday, Page & Company.

State Politics

Currently Hawaii has in place a system of universal health insurance through employer mandate. The fact that this reform was attainable in Hawaii is revealing about the internal politics of the state. The relatively high union density in Hawaii combined with the centrality of organized industries in the state economy rendered progress on health care reform less difficult than on the national level. Organized employers did not seek to derail health care reform and there was no entrenched health insurance industry to obstruct change. Moreover, conservatives in state legislatures do not have the filibuster, the right wing's powerful weapon in the Senate.

The so-called "Wisconsin Idea" exemplified an historical moment during the Progressive era in which social legislation was enacted, given public support and the absence of an effective business opposition. David Thelen's *Robert La Follette and the Insurgent Spirit* (1976) describes the mood of Wisconsin early in the century, when a widely shared sense of economic difficulty prepared the citizens of Wisconsin for aggressive measures to expand economic security. The cause of reform had substantial support even within the business community, since the depression had shaken business confidence in the status quo.

Oregon enacted a new health and safety program following discussions among employers and unionists early in the 1990s. Employers were prepared to accept a law that mandates health and safety committees in most workplaces in return for some relief from the burden of workers' compensation premiums. While similar laws have been or soon may be enacted in other states (sometimes with the support of the state Chamber of Commerce), business lobbies on the federal level are fiercely opposed to the concept of mandatory committees.

Thus, the prospects for social legislation vary a great deal by state. States with relatively powerful labor movements appear more receptive to social legislation. States with extremely weak labor movements tend to have regressive labor and social policies. Two legal issues that divide progressive from regressive jurisdictions are "right to work" and public-sector collective bargaining. Twenty-one states, largely in the south and west, have "right to work" laws prohibiting unions and employers from negotiating agreements that require the payment of dues for represented workers. Many of these same states lack any policy authorizing collective bargaining in the public sector. The presence of a "right to work" law and absence of public-sector collective bargaining legislation tend to be associated with reduced prospects for the enactment of other social legislation.

Consider Table 9.1 comparing the percentage of manufacturing workers organized by state. Michigan's manufacturing union density of 51.7 percent (in 1989; it has since declined further) is the highest, contrasting sharply with South Carolina's 2.95 percent and South Dakota's 2.34 percent. Broader measures of union density reveal a some-

Table 9.1
Percentage of Manufacturing Workers Unionized (1989)

State	% Union
Alabama	14.47
Alaska	24.66
Arizona	3.69
Arkansas	11.28
California	22.37
Colorado	9.57
Connecticut	15.35
Delaware	19.38
Florida	8.97
Georgia	11.82
Hawaii	41.36
Idaho	7.36
Illinois	29.82
Indiana	37.02
Iowa	18.64
Kansas	11.01
Kentucky	21.52
Louisiana	19.45
Maine	18.34
Massachusetts	19.66
Michigan	51.70
Minnesota	16.69
Mississippi	7.81
Missouri	29.75
Montana	22.79
Nebraska	8.70

State	% Union
Nevada	5.36
New Hampshire	6.66
New Jersey	24.38
New Mexico	9.44
New York	47.23
North Carolina	4.46
North Dakota	9.70
Ohio	39.76
Oklahoma	16.02
Oregon	20.41
Pennsylvania	39.32
Rhode Island	11.06
South Carolina	2.95
South Dakota	2.34
Tennessee	12.86
Texas	13.89
Utah	4.47
Vermont	7.98
Virginia	11.94
Washington	25.36
West Virginia	28.41
Wisconsin	23.06
Wyoming	13.83

Source: Grant Thornton 1990, p. 160.

what smaller variance across the states. (Reliable figures are difficult to find because the U.S. Bureau of Labor Statistics no longer supplies state data.)

The source of the table is itself revealing. For eleven years, Grant Thornton, a management consulting firm, evaluated the manufacturing climate in each state according to variables identified by associations of manufacturers. Labor costs, union density, and the burden of regulation were principal concerns of the manufacturers. (Public criticism of the underlying logic of these ratings led the firm to cease publishing them after 1990.)

The Grant Thornton ratings illustrate the resistance of many employers to unionism and social legislation, since the ratings discourage employers from locating in states with relatively high density and progressive laws. The Chamber of Commerce and National Association of Manufacturers also advise members about the question of "business climate," which, in itself, embodies the associations' unwillingness to compromise with labor and other stakeholder groups and reveals the wide variance in state responsiveness to stakeholders (Grant Thornton 1990, p. 160).

REFERENCES

Grant Thornton. (1990). *Eleventh annual Grant Thornton manufacturing climates study*. Chicago: Grant Thornton.

Thelen, D. (1976). *Robert M. La Follette and the insurgent spirit*. Boston: Little, Brown.

CHAPTER TEN

Think Tanks and Political Rhetoric

BUSINESS-ORIENTED THINK TANKS

The business lobbies in many cases work closely with think tanks supported by the business community. The philosophy of the Heritage Foundation is based on Austrian economics, on the work of Ludwig Von Mises, Frederic von Hayek, and their disciples. These writers combined a commitment to laissez faire capitalism with a distrust of democratic government. The Heritage Foundation adds to Austrian economics a cultural strategy: an attack on liberal leaders as simultaneously elitist and permissive. Writer Michael Lind calls this "culture-war politics" and describes it as an effort to disguise the class content of pro-corporate politics (1996, pp. 11–12).

The Heritage Foundation's philosophical roots in Austrian economics seldom lead to any conflict with the NAM or Chamber of Commerce or with the somewhat more moderate think tank, the American Enterprise Institute (AEI). Both Heritage and the libertarian Cato Institute have released reports critical of corporate subsidies as inconsistent with free market principles. AEI would be less likely to emphasize such a strategy. All three think tanks ordinarily publish reports that are critical of the welfare state and supportive of deregulation and are thus helpful to the business lobbies.

I interviewed a staffer at the Heritage Foundation, a former left-wing Democrat, who revealed some of the assumptions that guide the work of Heritage. Like many conservatives, he argued that inequality is an "engine" of free society. Those who protest inequality, he insisted, only demonstrate their own envy. He claimed that his true constituency was small business—for example, Korean grocers in poor neighborhoods, braving community hostility, crime, and the burdens of regulation, to provide for their families. He denied that the Heritage Foundation was beholden to the Olin Foundation, AmWay, or to the Coors family, or even that it was primarily an advocate of business interests. He attributed his own conservatism to concern over the rise of illegitimacy and the injustice of affirmative action. He reserved special scorn for those who perceive themselves as "victims," whether women, members of minority groups, or the poor. Note that there is no acknowledgment in this philosophy of any injustices emerging from the operations of markets.

The embrace of markets is implicit endorsement of a logic of exclusion. In the marketplace, there are inevitably losers, and laissez-faire consigns the losers to the margins of society. Mark Wilson of the Heritage Foundation once shocked my students with his apparent disdain for the jobless, implying that, if they were hungry, it was their just punishment.[1]

The hostility of organized business today to the labor movement is reflected in Max Green's *Epitaph for American Labor* (1996), a polemic by a former trade unionist published by the American Enterprise Institute. Green seeks to convince the reader that John Sweeney's leadership of the AFL-CIO completes a process of leftward drift that began under Lane Kirkland if not earlier, and that the result is a movement out of touch with American values. Green is not content with this line of attack alone. He also hopes to demonstrate that the more conservative, anti-communist AFL-CIO of George Meany (as well as the AFL of Samuel Gompers) was effective neither in its anti-communism nor in its bread and butter collective bargaining.

The significance of this book is that it reveals trends in the conservative movement. Green received financial assistance from the conservative Bradley and Smith Richardson Foundations, and the book itself was published by the American Enterprise Institute Press. While some conservatives have written favorably of the American labor movement, citing labor as a bulwark against revolution, Green and the conservatives he represents have apparently decided to renounce labor altogether.

Green considers the historic philosophies of American labor in order to prove that the AFL of Samuel Gompers contained the seeds of radicalism. He laments Gompers' departures from free market orthodoxy. He decries labor's growing commitment to government activism in economics (already evident in George Meany's AFL-CIO). He admits the anti-communism of Gompers, David Dubinsky, and other labor leaders but submits (pp. 7–8): "just as labor's ability to raise wages was more apparent than real, so was the part it played in the West's victory in the cold war more myth than fact."

The reader will discover that Green's problem is not with Sweeney's apparently more militant labor movement but with organized labor itself. Green would have the AFL-CIO abandon any critique of free markets. He condemns labor for its opposition to free trade and advocacy of trade unionism elsewhere in the world.

For the author, it is self-evident that the economic success of the Four Little Dragons—Hong Kong, Singapore,

South Korea, and Taiwan—has depended upon low-wage, controlled labor strategies. Here Green demonstrates no concern about the plight of workers under authoritarian regimes. He apparently finds no contradiction between his embrace of the dragons and their sometimes repressive regimes and his commitment to the ideal of "free" markets.

Green next indicts labor for its domestic policies. He insists that the AFL-CIO has capitulated to civil rights leaders in its support for affirmative action, that the federation has inappropriately attributed ghetto riots to social causes, and that it has wrongly argued for welfare as a right. The public sector unions earn harsh words for opposing privatization, and Green's former employer, the American Federation of Teachers, is faulted for favoring Head Start.

Green claims that the AFL-CIO has made common cause with cultural radicals and the New Left. He apparently rejects the notion that such steps as favoring affirmative action and opposing privatization might represent responses to internal union constituencies.

The concluding chapter of *Epitaph for American Labor* is a jumble of arguments. Its apparent purpose is to finally dispose of any remaining arguments for union legitimacy. Green favorably quotes economists who deny that unions raise workers' wages and insists that gains for workers have come from businesses' voluntary actions. He denies that labor's difficulties in organizing derive in any significant respect from employer opposition. Green's polemical maneuvers are well illustrated here. Initially he questions research that suggests that workers are routinely fired for attempting to organize unions (p. 159). Then he reports a study by Robert LaLonde and Bernard Meltzer that finds intentional discharges in perhaps 30 percent of all organizing campaigns. Having conceded this, Green suggests that firing organizers may actually increase the union's chances of winning the election. Thus frequent intentional discharges provide no basis for criticism of employer behavior.

John Hood's *The Heroic Enterprise: Business and the Common Good* is a polemic against socially responsible business, funded by conservative foundations. The author blames government regulators rather than business for a tragic fire in a poultry processing plant that killed over twenty employees. While Hood concedes that management locked the plant doors from the outside, he alleges that this was an effort to comply with other government regulations. Hood reserves his scorn both for agents of government and for business leaders who argue for generosity to stakeholders beyond the dictates of markets.

Corporations practice philanthropy for a variety of reasons. First, they derive benefit in public prestige for charitable giving. Second, corporate leaders may approve of the social goals of the organizations to which they provide assistance. Third, they may hope to influence these organizations. Finally, corporate leaders may seek tax advantages through giving.

Many corporations provide funds to a variety of concerns with disparate values and politics. For example, the Ford Motor Company has contributed to the American Lung Association, which favors higher emissions standards, while also supporting conservative think tanks with an antiregulatory message. Ford executives have determined that the company's reputation is improved by contributions to the American Lung Association despite the latter's public policy goals.

Many in the mainstream business lobbies are opposed to corporate philanthropy that benefits so-called "public interest groups," non-profits with causes that justify regulation of corporations. In this they have an ally: the Capital Research Center (CRC). CRC annually publishes *Patterns of Corporate Philanthropy: Funding Enemies, Forsaking Friends* with this end:

Capital Research Center's decade of research is meant to show American business the dangers of funding advocacy groups that distrust capitalism and favor government solutions to social problems. Such support hurts true charity and its beneficiaries, because public services discourage contributions to the private and voluntary sectors. Misguided giving also hurts stockholders, a top priority for corporations. (Capital Research Center 1997)

The CRC is an agent of discipline for the corporate community, and its work embodies a contradiction. Conservatives value employer discretion, but the CRC would have corporations abandon their strategic approaches to philanthropy if they contradict the CRC's rigid ideology.

POLITICAL RHETORIC

The experience of Nazism and fascism has led many political scientists and social philosophers to become concerned with the political use of language. The Nazis used language to divide the German people, to characterize segments of the population in dehumanizing or aggrandizing ways. The business lobbies have also manipulated language for political purposes in the United States, as have other political movements. This section will focus on efforts by organized business to undermine the appeal of the welfare state and social legislation through rhetorical devices.

Roger Brown, an eminent psychologist, demonstrates how language establishes hierarchies or an order of classes. He refers to the historical evaluation of European pronouns of address and classifies these as T vs V; T meaning "tu" and V meaning "vous." The relationship between T and V is that T always defers to V, or V is the superior and T the inferior. V would be the authority; T would be the recipient of that authority. Thus, hierarchy is deeply embedded in such languages as French and German. Linguistically, who the authority is and the direction of the authority are evident (Brown 1965, pp. 54–55).

Klemperer made a fascinating study of the Nazis' "measure of language." He wrote that the "Nazis despoiled the German language with the same unrelenting thoroughness that they applied to human and material resources, deprived it of all grace, subtlety and multiformity." Kemperer claimed that Nazis used words as harpoons against the subconscious. Their speech was incantatory and inciteful, dehumanizing, sentimentalizing, and euphemistic. Also, according to Kemperer, Nazi speech tended to be heavy with superlatives (Grunberger 1971, pp. 356–357, 363).

One of the Nazi programs was to promote a particular form of address, that is, "sie" for white collar workers, and "du" for those to be less respected. So white collar workers were to be addressed as "sie"; blue as "du." This program apparently did not work out although its authoritarian nature is obvious (Grunberger 1971, p. 215).

Craig (1983, p. 320) writes that "the establishment of the German Empire in 1871 subjected the [German] language to new strains that arose from the changed political conditions." He credits the Prussian Army as being a unifying force and finds that the language could not escape its influence. Metaphors of power began to abound in newspaper writing, parliamentary speeches, and university lectures. Spoken language combined influences from the garrison and the casino "because it seemed to be the style of a superior caste . . . and seemed to connote qualities of decisiveness and moral force."

The Nazi party required a militant language; words like *Schlat, Einsatz, Einhet, Front*, and *Durchbruch* were borrowed from the vocabulary of the army. Superlatives and enhancing adjectives became more and more frequent: for example, *einmalig* (unique); *historisch* (historical); *Welt,* (world); and *gross* (great) (Craig 1983, pp. 322–323).

Under the Nazis, the German language was altered to help change the way the German people thought about politics. The desired topics of conversation, the desired words and phrases were promoted by all branches of government, the educational system and the ministry of propaganda.

The Nazis have not been the only ones to attempt to destroy a people's ability to choose their own vocabulary and to think independently. The Soviets behaved in similar ways.

Linguists and anthropologist-linguists have arrived at a deterministic formula that stipulates not that culture determines language but that language determines culture. Benjamin Whorf studied the languages of the Indians of the Southwest and remarked upon the absence of terms for gender. The Eskimos developed many different ways of describing snow. To paraphrase Whorf, thought is molded by syntax and vocabulary or language shapes or influences what we see and think (Pinker 1995, pp. 536–537).

In the United States, business lobbies have been working hard since World War II to repeal the New Deal and later the Great Society. The leaders of the NAM and Chamber of Commerce denounced the New Deal as socialist or communist. More recently, "socialist" and "communist" have lost some of their effect, for which reason business advocates have increasingly focused on the repudiation of liberalism. The word "liberal" in American political discourse has been made noxious by definition, example, and pronunciation. It is used as an epithet by Republican politicians close to the business lobbies. The Republican attack on this word has been so successful that Democrats are fearful of using it.

Another phrase that is commonly used by business lobby leaders is "big government." Sometimes it is embellished as "failed liberal, big-government solutions." The opposition to Clinton's health care reform initiative used this language to good effect. "Big government" is a transparently deceptive phrase because most individuals from the left, right, and center favor robust government action in one arena or another. It is a phrase whose purpose is to generate reflexive responses and discourage analysis.

There are examples in which a word is used to convey the opposite of its usually accepted meaning. House Speaker Newt Gingrich was one of the founders of the Conservative Opportunity Society. A review of the programs proposed by this group will demonstrate that their concern is increased opportunity for entrepreneurs but perhaps diminished opportunity for others.

"Tell Newt to Shut Up," by Maraniss and Weisskopf (1996, pp. 128–145), provides details of Gingrich's approach to political rhetoric. (The authors fail to mention management consultant Maurice Schecter, who has been particularly helpful to Gingrich in this project.) CommStrat was a team of public relations professionals who assisted the Republicans in choices of rhetoric in the 1995 campaign to reduce spending on Medicare in order to fund tax cuts and balance the budget. Although the Republican plan would slowly compromise the universality and benefit levels of Medicare, party tacticians and their business lobby allies wanted to avoid a backlash from seniors. CommStrat and other consultants recommended that Republicans propose to "preserve, protect, and improve" Medicare. Democrats who noted that the Republicans' approach to the "preservation" of medicare involved substantial cuts were accused by Republicans and many commentators of "demagoging" the issue. This last term appears to be a new invention.

Gingrich has frequently asserted that liberals and Democrats were responsible for the threatened decline of American civilization. This appears to be a modification of a rhetorical strategy often invoked by the southern right in their defense of Bourbon dominance. Slave-owners and the employers of tenant farmers and other near slaves follow-ing the Civil War were inclined to attack critics of the social order by insisting that the survival of the "southern way of life" was at stake.

NOTE

1. Presentation to class by Mark Wilson of the Heritage Foundation at Cornell Center, Washington, D.C., February 10, 1997. See also George (1997).

REFERENCES

Brown, R. (1965). *Social psychology*. New York: The Free Press.

Craig, G. A. (1983). *The German*. New York: New American Library.

George, S. (1997). "How to win the war of ideas: Lessons from the Gramscian Right." *Dissent*: 47–53.

Green, M. (1996). *Epitaph for American labor: How union leaders lost touch with America*. Washington, D.C.: AEI Press.

Grunberger, F. V. (1980). *Prophets without honor*. New York: McGraw-Hill.

Hood, J. M. (1996). *The heroic enterprise: Business and the common good*. New York: The Free Press.

Lind, M. (1996). *Up from conservatism: Why the right is wrong for America*. New York: The Free Press.

Maraniss, D., and M. Weisskopf (1996). *"Tell Newt to shut up."* New York: Touchstone.

Pinker, S. (1995). *The language instinct*. New York: HarperCollins.

Values and Business Schools

One potential but unlikely source of critical thinking in business is the business school. Business schools' curricula tend to reinforce the isolation of managers. The substance of courses and the prevailing culture reinforce the view that managers are a distinct class who are appropriately focused on self-enrichment. Their "professionalism" and entrepreneurial values distinguish them from non-managers.

Neoclassical assumptions are central to most of the disciplines of the business school. Courses in finance implicitly uphold the rationality and positive results of private capital markets. Courses in marketing necessarily endorse corporate investments in manipulation at the possible expense of production. Very seldom is a course taught in such a way as to stimulate creative thinking as to the benefits and deficiencies of the corporate status quo. Instructors who attempt this receive critical evaluations from many students who want nothing more than the skills and knowledge that are strategic to advancement on the job.

Sociologist Amitai Etzioni writes:

The curriculum of numerous business schools is heavily influenced by neoclassical economics that stresses rationality . . . , market considerations, and profit-making. Students are also provided with some classes in psychology, human resources, and more recently and in fewer schools, with classes on business and government and society. . . . The content of these classes is often not compatible with the others because very often they build on conflicting assumptions about human nature and society. (Etzioni 1991, pp. 360–361)

Faculty in the industrial relations/human resources and business and society disciplines are most likely to be the dissenters from the business school orthodoxy. Studies by John Godard (1995) illustrate the more critical views of business, including support for unions, that characterize the first group. Business and society instructors may be somewhat more sympathetic to environmental regulation. Despite these pockets of dissent, business schools are likely to reinforce students' inclinations to uncritically accept management authority.

In his book *Beyond Individualism*, Piore (1995, pp. 131–132) criticizes the social isolation of identity groups in American society. He decries the difficulties that arise when individuals of different races, sexual preferences, or disabilities are incapable of mutual understanding. He worries that "the politics of the new identity groups is creating a set of self-absorbed worlds in which citizens speak increasingly to others like themselves and there is less and less conversation across group boundaries." Managers appear to constitute an identity group with a very limited capacity to converse with other groups in society. The market model contributes to this problem in its imposition of the concept of predictable transactions on most social processes, and business schools socialize prospective managers in this misunderstanding.

A manager who insists that he can unilaterally determine a just contract for employees seems to discount the social structure of knowledge. This misconception is linked to neoclassical economics, which are fundamentally deductive in nature. The market model allows one to deduce an appropriate wage rate for employees without a process of joint deliberations that advance the employer's and workers' knowledge of one another. In the philosophy of John Dewey, the democratic process within unions and the practice of bargaining advance the "social intelligence," which is superior to any unilaterally derived knowledge.

Edward Filene conjectured that the reason why many successful leaders of business remain conservative is that "they do not, as a rule, have enough social and recreational contacts with men of other classes, other interests, and other points of view" (1924, p. 292). Filene proposed that there be clubs in each community in which the rich and poor, the radical and conservative, would meet one another. The business school as it is usually designed certainly does little to serve such a function.

I interviewed faculty at a U.S. business school and found among many of them a limited and contingent acceptance of some businesses' efforts to address stakeholder needs:

Well, you know, I think you can survive [as an altruist], but what I think is interesting is that I don't think you'll be liked very much. I don't think it makes someone very popular, the more altruistic and the nicer you are to others. . . . I think that the people that they help sometimes don't like them because they somewhat resent them giving the help. And I think other people don't like them because they don't understand them because they're so focused on their own, you know, greed or selfishness. . . .

Some, some amount of altruism [works in business], but I think it has to be balanced altruism. I mean, I think, I do believe that businesses can do good. And I really, actually I think that doing good by businesses, having a social conscience will benefit them in the long run. I mean, I think it's very shortsighted to think that you can use up all the resources or whatever and then, you know, fare well. So if you do take a long view, then you probably will think about doing a lot of things that will benefit humanity.[1]

I found that faculty acceptance of social responsibility in business is often contingent on market success. Many business school faculty confidently proclaim the essential compatibility of social responsibility and profits. Few concede that the solution of social programs might legitimately require sacrifice of profits and other significant concessions to stakeholders.

NOTE

1. Interview with Professor Nancy Bagranoff, American University, Washington, D.C., August 15, 1997.

REFERENCE

Etzioni, A. (1991). "Reflections on teaching of business ethics." *Business Ethics Quarterly*: 355–365.

Filene, E. A. (1924). *The way out: A forecast of coming changes in American business and industry*. Garden City, N.Y.: Doubleday, Page & Company.

Godard, J. (1995). "The ideologies of Canadian and U.S. scholars." *Journal of Labor Research*: 127–148.

Piore, M. (1995). *Beyond individualism*. Cambridge, Mass.: Harvard University Press.

_____

CHAPTER TWELVE

A Conservative View

Professor Kathleen Getz, who teaches the discipline of Business and Society at the Kogod College of Business Administration at American University, and I have compared liberal and conservative views of the market in conversation.[1] I found her, like many business school professors, to be critically supportive of the positions of the business lobbies on such issues as social security and the role of the government in the economy.

Jacobs: If one loses in the marketplace, if one is poor . . . what does that mean about the people who lose? What are their qualities?

Getz: This is a funny question. We were just talking about this in class today . . . [the] history of wealth [as a] laudable goal . . . the theological justification and the scientific "Social Darwinism. . . ." My view is that losing in the market place cannot be treated, in the end, as one particular thing. There is always a big chunk of pure luck in whether one succeeds or loses: being in the "right place at the right time." There's also: are you born without the stuff the marketplace rewards? In other words, do you have the level of intellect, some talent, some physical feature that the marketplace rewards, or don't you? And that is a form of luck, too. There is the background, again, luck . . . who are your parents, and what kind of upbringing did you have and were you exposed to the kinds of things that create opportunities? But it also does say something about the person . . . how hard a person has worked. Not everybody succeeds in the marketplace through luck. A lot of people succeed through hard work. But in saying luck plays a role in losing, you also must say that luck plays a role in winning, but it is not the only part of winning or losing. People who lose in the marketplace, some of them, but not all of them, may be lazy. Some of them, but not all of them, may be on the lower end of the intelligence scale, whichever form of intelligence you measure (because there are so many different kinds). And some of them are just plain unlucky. I don't think it says, necessarily, something about the quality of the person, but it may. And to assume the winners are good, hard-working people and the losers are bad, lazy people is not a good assumption. And I don't think that you can [make that assumption]. I don't think you know anything about a person by just looking at their success or lack of it in the marketplace. To see that somebody is poor or wealthy doesn't tell you much about the person, so I don't think that it says that much about a person by itself.

Jacobs: The Social Security system to some degree distributes income and insulates some sections of the poor from the worst consequences of their "failure." Does a system that establishes a floor for the needy properly or improperly interfere with the forces of the marketplace?

Getz: A system that establishes a floor for the needy properly interferes with the workings of the marketplace. There are some people who would disagree with that statement, and would think that I am not very conservative for saying that. I think where I disagree with people who are more liberal than me—not more conservative but more liberal—is what that floor would be and how it would be established. But failure in the marketplace, whether it is your own fault or the fault of your parents or dumb luck, shouldn't condemn people to a life of extreme deprivation. Just as other kinds of failures . . . we all fail at this, that or the other occasionally . . . doesn't condemn us for the rest of our lives, marketplace failure should not condemn a person to deprivation.

Jacobs: The main organizations that represent business—the Chamber of Commerce, the National Association of Manufacturers, the National Federation of Independent Businesses, groups of that kind . . . have consistently opposed Social Security. They opposed the introduction of Social Security and now they are calling for the privatization of Social Security. . . . Do you favor privatization?

Getz: Yes. I oppose Social Security and I think privatization is a halfway point to getting to where we need to be. I think people ought to save their money to the extent they can for later in life. I don't think that the government should tell people how much they should save or where they should save it. So privatization would get the government out of saying where they must save it, or how they must save it. It would not get the government out of saying how much they must save, and abolishing Social Security would get the government out of saying how much ought to be saved. If Social Security is abolished and people are left to their own devices, there will be people who don't save for retirement, and I just said that people who through their own mistakes or for other reasons are desperately poor, should be helped. I still believe that, and so there will be people who don't save because they are extravagant, who don't save because they don't have enough money to save, who don't save because they don't have any foresight—whatever the reason, in the end the result will be they will need some help later on in life. I think that for those who are extravagant with their money and who don't save . . . they will be severely punished because they won't be living the extravagant life to which they have become accustomed; and as far as I am concerned, if there is a punishment needed for them for being extravagant, that is an adequate punishment. When I say that I favor some type of a system whereby there is a floor . . . is that what we called it before, a floor? . . . that suggests . . . Let me back up. I don't think that Social Security is the right system because it is based on retirement income and those kinds of things. I think that there is some kind of welfare system that is needed. My preference would be to have the government involved in that as little as possible, and my strongest preference would be to have the government out of that and have private institutions—churches, religious organizations primarily, but others as well—foundations—doing this kind of work. . . . I suspect that it wouldn't be sufficient and that the government will always need to be involved. But the less the government is involved in these kinds of things, the better.

Jacobs: What is the advantage in having the government less involved?

Getz: Freedom of choice, freedom for the people whose money is being used for different things.

Jacobs: Freedom of choice for the contributors, but less freedom of choice for the recipients.

Getz: The role of the government would be to provide for those for whom nobody else cares to provide.

Jacobs: But aren't you then increasing the prospects for groups of people failing to receive help from some system, because by focusing on selective [private contributions] you are increasing the loopholes in the system, aren't you?

Getz: Yeah, in a way I am. That is why I said the government would still have a role. I have difficulty imagining a system that would be satisfactory where the government didn't play a role, because there will be types of people, groups of people, that are not helped through private initiative for whatever reason. But I think in the ideal world as I would like it to be, that we could have a lot of help going to people that doesn't have to go through the government. The advantage—I didn't answer this question—the advantage to having the government not involved is simply an advantage related to efficient use of money—that the money doesn't get run through yet another layer of bureaucracy and have some of it siphoned off for administrative uses rather than for the good that it can do.

Jacobs: . . . when I've heard comparisons of the efficiency of public and private systems, I've always been told that in the administration of Social Security, and [in the] administration of programs like Medicare . . . that you find much less overhead in the public system. When you have large monopolies there are certain large economies of scale, there is less expense in advertising. What are the kinds of efficiencies that you think a privately administered welfare system provides?

Getz: Well, the first point is that this is what I think and not what I know. I don't have any data to support this. There are arguments related to monopolies and efficiencies that monopolies can enjoy, but they have to be balanced with arguments related to the lack of necessity to be efficient if you are a monopoly. You are not competing with anyone and so there is no incentive to be efficient. I visualize private initiatives where there would be some competition for the donors' money and there may be advertising necessary—in the society in which we live probably way more than I would like that there be. I guess it is almost an article of faith for me that competition drives efficiency, that having a single system, Medicare, Medicaid, Social Security, creates opportunities for waste.

Jacobs: [Economist Albert] Hirshman (1970) says that there is always slack in organizations, and inefficiencies, so there are two ways people discuss remedying those deficiencies. One is leaving, and that is the marketplace remedy . . . generat[ing] the greater efficiencies [through] voluntary behavior in a competitive environment, but then there is also the opportunity to improve an organization by voice. Now that is what is presumably available to us in a system that is democratic-governmental. So why is it that you are . . . convinced of the virtues of competition as a way of promoting efficiencies, but don't seem to consider voice an adequate remedy?

Getz: Perhaps because I haven't ever seen any evidence that voice works. Based on anecdotal evidence rather than scientific, it certainly appears to me that the person who works in the monopolistic system who thinks that things can be done more effectively, has a difficult time having his voice heard. There is a certain lethargy that you must first deal with in monopolistic organizations. There is no need to change at all, and certainly no need to change quickly. The fact is that there is no need to be responsive.

Jacobs: You are . . . sort of denying anything that has happened in the past two hundred centuries in the development of democratic institutions. Does a democratic institution mean anything in terms of the responsiveness to the people?

Getz: Oh sure, democratic institutions mean plenty. Do you think the Social Security administration is democratic?

Jacobs: No, I think perhaps that the Social Security administration is a legitimate creation of the people through the state, and it is reasonable for the people to say we can more generously provide for people in difficult circumstances if we pool our income and give up individual choice in terms of linking [a donor] to a beneficiary, but we will instead have a lot of money available for solving problems.

Getz: Do you think that is why the Social Security administration was formed? Or how it was formed?

Jacobs: That is an interesting question. . . . there was a great deal of pressure from the grassroots, people who were old and incapable of working, and there was a mass movement for something called the Townsend Plan which would have been very generous and not well designed, and that pressure, and other forms of pressure, led to Congress acting . . . [to] be sure that people in their old age don't have to work.

Getz: But if you look at the system today, there are lots of people who have legitimate interests in the Social Security system, right? Everybody who participates in it, which is almost everybody in the country. Some people's interest in the Social Security system is more immediate than others because they are currently recipients of Social Security and others are not. When issues related to Social Security are discussed in the political arena those of us for whom it is less immediately important tend to not get involved in those discussions. Those who are more immediately involved . . . essentially the beneficiaries of the system, tend to be more involved in the discussion, tend to be more politically active . . . and so what happens is that the somewhat smaller group that benefits speaks more loudly than the somewhat larger group that is not currently benefiting and of course a lot of us, not all of us—but a lot of us—don't think we ever will benefit, or certainly don't think we will get our money's worth out of it. But we are not involved, we don't have any sense of "now" to be involved. A classic problem where the small group that is noisy gets its way rather than the big group that stays quiet.

Jacobs: I'm intrigued by that analysis . . . I feel that I have an immediate interest in Social Security because my parents live down the street. Their incomes depend upon it, and my life is very much influenced by that. I think that, I know that, business lobbies and many conservatives characterize the response of elder groups to any proposed cut in Social Security as well . . . they talk about the issue being "demagogued," and in a way [that is how] you have described it . . . [you've implied] there is something sinister about the way one group is able to control the issues, when to me it seems Social Security succeeds because it has wide public support, not just the support of the elderly.

Getz: First off, I do think that there is a lot of demagoguery that goes on. It is partly a result of the political system we have, in large part a result of the media that we have which does not explore any issue in any great depth but just kind of picks out little parts of them. Your interest in Social Security is greater than mine, because your parents are recipients right now, mine are not. Will it interest me when my parents become recipients? Probably. I don't think my parents will get enough on Social Security to survive. In fact, my mother has declined to retire because they won't get enough on Social Security to survive. And in that sense I know that my sisters and I are going to be contributing to my parents' income, and my cynical response to that is, well, what good has Social Security done my parents? My father worked for how many years, my mother worked for quite a number of years and still works, and they're going to get Social Security and it's not going to provide for them. Had they had the money to invest themselves, from what I've read, they could have invested and earned more money than they're going to get from Social Security . . . that the market place return is greater than the Social Security return. . . .

Jacobs: . . . I am interested in your assessment of the legitimacy of governmental action and the legitimacy of private voluntary action and the character of corporate behavior in this context. In your description of . . . Social Security in the [campaign] for privatization, one scenario you didn't . . . emphasize was privatization as windfall for the investment community.

Getz: It would be, it would be.

Jacobs: So, in other words, when you look at the whole political scenario you see the elderly groups unfairly manipulating the politics of it and the media failing to illuminate the problem. When I look at it I see the right wing, after decades and decades of failing to eliminate the [Social Security] system, finally perceiving the opportunity to do so. It is not because people have been ignorant about the potential of the alternatives, it is because people have legitimately fought to maintain the system. So, that said, I am always intrigued by those different ways you might perceive those sorts of problems.

Getz: I think that we all go into it with some kind of a bias, and we sort of look at the facts and highlight different ones, but you're highlighting the past and current activities of the investment community, which does stand to gain a windfall if Social Security is privatized, whereas I am highlighting the past and current activities of the elderly groups and saying that they have prevented something from happening through their activities. It is . . . who do we see as having legitimacy, and you see the elderly groups as being representative of a larger segment of the population. I don't see the investment community as representing the rest of us. I see their interests as coinciding with the rest of us that . . . but they are certainly not our representatives. . . .

Jacobs: When I was interviewing Ed Potter of the Labor Policy Association, he said that too much labor law . . . assumes that managers are bad people out to exploit their employees. He said on the other hand that the vast majority of the CEOs at Fortune 500 companies really want to do the right thing. They want to act the righteous way. Do you think that that is an accurate characterization of the behavior of chief executives . . . to what degree are they prone to abuse their power?

Getz: I think that it is human nature for us to be prone to abuse whatever measure of power we have. I also think that most managers would prefer to do the right thing, if they knew what it was, or if they thought they could legitimately take the time to think about it. My guess is that not very many CEOs think very frequently about their workers, that they are thinking about grand strategies and not thinking about the individual person working on the line or wherever that person happens to be working. But if they do take the time to think about it, I think that they are more likely to have the kind of thoughts that I would consider the right ones as opposed to the wrong ones. I don't think that they have a natural inclination to be abusive of their workers. I think it really helps in institutions or organizations when workers are viewed as people, where the CEO has actually been face to face with workers, for example, and the humanizing aspect of that is very important. But I think that the inclination . . . that CEOs would rather do the right thing. I don't think that they are necessarily righteous, but I think that their preference would be to do the right thing rather than to make the extra buck.

Jacobs: . . . the late theologian Reinhold Niebuhr (1944) wrote a book called *The Children of Light and The Children of Darkness*. I found part of it very interesting. . . . He said that . . . the left and the right have both been guilty of an illusion that people in power can be trusted to do good. That, on the part of the left, [the assumption that] those with the power of revolution would not harm the citizens [was] wrong. . . . [many leftists] were naïve, and ultimately they were cynical as well when they [rationalized revolutionary excesses]. Niebuhr said similarly that those on the right who believe the leaders of large corporations really will not abuse their power and that in the marketplace exploitation is not endemic, that those sorts of people are also naïve. Their naïvete about the use and abuse of power leads also to a kind of cynicism [in] which people justify and tolerate the use and abuse of power by private organizations. I am quite intrigued by how private elites may abuse their power. What can you do about it?

Getz: What kind of problem is it? A real problem. It is a problem of private abuse and public abuse, of public elites and private elites. The old saying [that] power corrupts is one of those old sayings that has some legitimacy. It is very easy to become detached from those over whom you have power. . . .

My recent [struggle over] tenure pointed this out to me, that power corrupts . . . a person sometimes fails to recognize how their power can affect other people, and so I never think of myself as a particularly powerful person, but when I went through this tenure thing ... I put myself in the position of the students and, being the professor, I have the same type of power over those students that the administration here has over me. My experience has led me to be less arbitrary, or to be careful about being arbitrary, in refusing or accepting requests from students and that kind of thing. I try to think more carefully about those kinds of things, and I had lost touch with that level of power that I had. I failed to recognize it for a while and now I have been reminded, and I'll probably eventually forget again, but I think that public and private elites fail to recognize the impact that their actions have on other people. Maybe it is naïvete. I don't think they want to do the wrong thing. I don't think they necessarily have ideas about being righteous, and wanting to do the right thing or be good, but I think they want to avoid doing the wrong thing.

Sometimes wanting to avoid doing the wrong thing can lead you into doing the right thing. There is a real concern, though. There is a lot of power in governmental officials. There is a lot of power in private organization officials. The kinds of stuff ... being revealed now about the president of the Teamsters Union [with respect to campaign irregularities] shows that it is in those kinds of organizations as well. The only way that I can think of to constrain that potential for abuse of power is watchdogs of one sort or another. The way the founders of our country set up a system whereby the three branches of government are supposed to watch over each other, we have evolved a system whereby the government watches over the private sector and some folks do some watching over the government. These folks who do the watching emerge rather than being democratically elected or assigned. But I don't think that we can rely entirely, and I hate to say it, but I don't think we can rely entirely upon peoples' own consciences to prevent them from abusing power. You are going to find bad people in positions of power as well as good people.

Jacobs: The [conservative group] Capital Research Center has gotten some publicity the past few years because they issue reports on philanthropy from corporations and they advise corporations to change their philanthropic practices. ... an example of what they seek to end is the Ford Corporation's contribution to the American Lung Association. This is their argument: the American Lung Association pretends to be a health oriented group but, in fact, [campaigns for] higher auto emissions standards. Therefore a corporation that contributes to this sort of group is shooting itself in the foot and undermining the free enterprise system. In corporate philanthropy is it appropriate for corporations to contribute to organizations which defend the free enterprise system, or are there also legitimate organizations of other kinds to which they can contribute [in the service of their] social responsibility?

Getz: I think that corporations can contribute to whomever they want. It's philanthropy, give-away. They can give away to whomever the team that's elected or appointed to make decisions for the organization decides to give. And the people at the . . . Capital Research Center can publicize and let other people know what their take on it is. . . . if the Ford Corporation wants to give to the American Lung Association, they can. Should they know that the American Lung Association lobbies to reduce emissions from automobiles? Well, that's a good thing to know. They should know what the groups that receive their money are doing, but the Lung Association is a health organization and they would be wrong not to lobby for emissions controls.

Jacobs: . . . the Capital Research Center's decade of research is meant to show Americans the dangers of funding advocacy groups that [combat] capitalism and favor government solutions to social problems. . . .

Getz: Well, the Capital Research Center is allowed to promote that kind of thing. I don't entirely agree with them. I don't entirely disagree with them. I think that . . . I would just as soon that they were simply disclosers of information rather than advocates of some sort, which they appear to be. But, as far as I'm concerned, to say that a corporation cannot give money to a particular group because that particular group does things that are inconsistent with the private enterprise system . . . Many of the other things that corporations do . . . are not consistent with the free enterprise system. Corporations don't walk the walk of private enterprise, they talk the talk, but they don't walk the walk because as soon as they can get some government legislation, they are lobbying for it, and that is not consistent with the private enterprise system. As long as we have a system, and I don't see it ending, whereby each individual organization seeks its own self-interests through whatever means it can, you are going to have corporations not promoting the private enterprise system. . . . Because every time a corporation asks the government for a favor, for trade protection, for subsidies for this, that, or the other, that is destructive to the private enterprise system. I would like to see those things ended, but to suggest that this is a critical element in destroying the private enterprise system is missing a big part of the picture.

Jacobs: The Capital Research Center represents a segment, obviously, of the corporate community that is not only opposed to government intervention in the economy, but also wants to guide corporations in their private views . . . so they are, in a sense, arguing that . . . corporations that don't focus on profit maximizing, that don't focus on the right kind of private enterprise advocacy, should be challenged. I guess this sort of thing leads me to believe that there is power arrayed against power in the arena of corporate social responsibility. . . . In fact there are movements for or against, and this is representative of the significant segment of the corporate community that is saying not only are free markets better, but corporations also should not depart from the strictest free market principles.

Getz: . . . That may be what they're saying. I would like to see what their stance is on corporate welfare, because if they are going to argue that companies cannot spend their profits because it interferes with the private enterprise system, they should argue that companies cannot lobby for corporate welfare, which of course is not what companies call it when they lobby, but is what they are lobbying for. To be ideologically true, that is what they would have to do. And if they're saying that this is an ideological argument, then they should be true to their ideology. I think what I am saying is that there is more than one side of government intervention in the marketplace, and in the free enterprise system.

Sometimes it is beneficial to companies and sometimes it is not. And the same thing the government does will aid some companies and harm others. That is another reason why I would just as soon see a lot less government involvement: because the government ends up creating winners and losers in the marketplace through some of its actions. . . . There's something better about the marketplace in the aggregate. But I don't think you can only look at the aggregate. That would be what my article of faith is, that the aggregate will be better under a competitive free enterprise system, but if you stop looking at that point then you will miss some important things.

Jacobs: . . . I am still trying to make sense of the variety of views that advocates of free market economics have about human nature, about human beings. . . .You talked about the welfare system and what might be the best combination of government and private involvement. I thought that maybe in that system there would be a few more people [who] slipped through the cracks. . . . Susan George [1997] [has] said that inevitably in the market model there is . . . a law of exclusion . . . those people who fail in the marketplace, unless there is a radical constraint over the way the market operates, are marginalized. That private philanthropy not only allows some to exercise greater control over the lives of those people [who] fail in the marketplace, but that it doesn't really make them whole. . . .

Getz: No, I can counter that with the idea that public philanthropy, the social welfare system, also creates dependency and control, it's just who is doing the controlling. Would you rather have a government bureaucracy having the control or some private organization having the control? My suggestion is that if the government has a monopoly on the social welfare system then people who are dependent and under control have no other choices, whereas if the social welfare system is privatized in some way . . . the recipients of that, the dependent parties, might have some choices. They might be able to move from dependency on one institution to dependency on another institution. Furthermore, when it's private initiative, people are working with their own money. People are giving away their own money rather than when it is the government giving away other people's money. If I am giving away my own money I have an incentive to help the recipient of my money change his or her behavior. . . .

Jacobs: Or to control the actions of the recipient of that money, as well, because there is that [potential] control.

Getz: Do I want to keep on giving the money away, or do I want to keep the money for myself? I personally would rather keep the money for myself, so my incentive would be to help that person figure out a way they no longer need my money. . . . There are all kinds of people, and some are bad. And some people will use the fact that they make a donation to help somebody else against the person being helped. And then, in fact, you are not trying to help somebody but to in some way make [yourself] more powerful, to consolidate or increase [your] power. You have those folks out there, whether we are talking about a public or private system. There are all kinds of horror stories out there. I've done a lot of reading, in . . . public sector adoption [cases]: people just abusing the power that they have over the people who want to adopt babies because of the dependency in the relationship. The bureaucracy can create very attractive employment opportunities for people who want to exploit other people. You don't even have to be a wealthy person, you just have to get the job with the government to be able to exploit other people. In the private system you are going to have to have some money to give away to be able to exploit. That doesn't mean the exploitation is any better, it's just as bad. I don't think one system or the other is more conducive to exploitation or corruption.

Jacobs: But you say that they are equally open to corruption, but for some other set of reasons you prefer the private sector?

Getz: . . . it is the idea that not everybody who gives is exploitative or corrupt and that it is those of us who are the givers in a private system will have the incentive to help. You know, it is the old story, give a fish versus teaching how to fish. And so we'll have an incentive to teach them how to fish because we don't want to keep giving our money away to what we feel is a bottomless pit. If you are the recipient of the largesse rather than the donor, you may have, not absolutely will have, but you may have other opportunities, you may have other sources of donations. Whereas in the governmental system, when the government has the monopoly, that is less likely to be the case, especially since we have seen that since the government took over social welfare we have seen a decline in private giving. People's excuse is that I am not going to give money to this charity or that because I am already giving money to the government and the government is taking care of that kind of thing. So private giving has been reduced because taxes have been increased—this is people's logic anyway, because they are paying for those kinds of things through their taxes. And so the choices for the recipients of the money are reduced. Again, it is the idea of competing to get something done and the competition leading to a better array of alternatives.

Jacobs: . . . I have been trying to get at something that occurred to me reading a book by Kristen Monroe (1995) called *The Heart of Altruism* . . . She interviewed a variety of individuals who had risked their lives to save others, those who saved Jews in World War II, and a woman in the south who risked her life a number of times on behalf of civil rights, and a few other examples of very public spirited individuals . . . and tried to make sense of what distinguished their way of looking at the world. . . . she wanted to define altruism. She said that economists and [other] social scientists . . . had not successfully, had not satisfactorily defined altruism. What altruism meant to her ultimately was having an inclusive view of humanity that didn't make distinctions among people that would allow one to favor one group or another or choose one group as undeserving and help another. When the heroes and heroines she described acted, they did so without wondering about whether or not the individual that they helped, whether he or she was . . . deserving. I guess my question is [to] what degree do you divide the world into deserving or undeserving?

Getz: Probably more than I should. I guess you know that I have pretty strong ties to my religion, and my religion says that what makes a person deserving or undeserving is largely for God, not for us, to decide. We can judge people's behavior, but we should not judge people. That's what my religion says, and the ultimate way from refraining [from] judging other people is, kind of in the way you are talking about here, to help people without regard to anything except their need for help. I guess what I would say is, I wish I were less judgmental about those things on a personal level as well as in terms of my way of thinking about the world ideologically or professionally. All that said, I do think that judgments ought to be made; but when it comes to some of the really basic questions that you're getting at here, there does come a time to suspend judgment.... [There is] a need ... so great that it must ... be served. Where I would draw the line is probably different from where other people would draw the line. Should I provide help for somebody who is less well off than I am? That depends to me on how less well off that person is. And deserving and undeserving of what? Everybody deserves some basic level of material stuff, food, clothes and shelter, whatever you want to put on the list. Does everybody deserve to be wealthy? Probably not.

Jacobs: ... Edward Filene [argued that] one of the reasons ... why many successful businessmen are predisposed to a conservative, if not reactionary, point of view is that as a rule they do not have enough social and recreational contacts with "men" of other classes, other interests, other points of view.... First of all, is it a problem?

Getz: What he describes is absolutely true. I don't know when [his] book was written, but it is true today. There are some barriers that have been crossed.... First of all, we wouldn't use only the masculine pronoun today because the business person does have contact with both men and women. The business person has contact with people of more than one race, more than one ethnic background, but, in terms of social class, there is very much an isolation. It goes both ways. The poor are only around the poor, and the wealthy are only around the wealthy, and because of that we all have some misconceptions about what the other people are like. We fail to think of them, number one, as people who have the same yearnings, desires, feelings that we have, and we tend to think of them as "them," and I think that his reading of the situation is very well done. That is why I think that companies should have management by walking around, which is kind of a cliché, but where that happens there is a better relationship among workers and supervisors, because the people see each other as people. Playing baseball with people is a good thing to do because it breaks down some of the barriers, going out for happy hour is a good thing to do because it breaks down those barriers. . . .

Jacobs: . . . I argue that there are a number of factors that make problem-solving difficult in society. That business lobbies are organized in such a way that [reinforces barriers between groups and] prohibits dialog.

Getz: What about the other lobbies?

Jacobs: . . . there may be that problem as well. . . . the market model . . . , I believe, permits an organization to foreswear dialog. . . . the market [model] says that it is all a matter of individual choice, that the market will generate [just] outcomes. We are not obliged to look and meet a group and consult and come to agreement. We can hope that, we can imagine that, that the marketplace process will work itself out on its own. . . .

One of the things I wonder about . . . are business schools contributing to the problem because they don't have borderlands [where workers, managers, and other social groups engage in dialog]? When you study business at a business school do you really learn [about the possibilities of dialog]? We teach courses in which we talk about stakeholders, but do you really learn in the final analysis that there is anything to be gained by dialog, compromise . . . ?

Getz: You learn you are supposed to manage it. . . . to our students that means control. So you're supposed to control, and that turns into manipulat[ing] stakeholders so they don't create problems for you. I always have a question at the end of the final exam, which the students think is worth points but is not because the exam is worth 105 points, but I have a question that says something to the effect of how will this course be of use to you later on in your career? I've had more than one student imply that it will enable them to dance around problems instead of dealing with real issues, and I've had students—one student in particular, whom I will never forget—say that it taught him to get away with all the things they are not supposed to do. A very disconcerting response. So, yes, in the business school we do, probably without intending to, make the borderlands few and far between. And companies are doing this today too, not just the business schools. All this diversity talk . . . has gotten to the point where [many] students are deaf to it. . . . What students say, straight out, is that they're tired of hearing about diversity and they don't want to know other things. I think it's in part because we have given it a name and we've talked about it, and we've been very careful in how we talk about it, not to offend. In so doing we have not had any real discussion about the issue of diversity. I am not fond of the term diversity, but essentially that is what Filene is talking about, and I think that we need to talk about diversity in terms of social class, much more so than in terms of race or ethnicity or sex. Many of those things have been addressed through lawsuits that, believe it or not, I think may have been necessary at the time. I think they are probably not so necessary now. But in business school we encourage people to associate with people like themselves. That is partly because it is a university and it's a campus and it's self-contained. But we've made no effort . . . I think it is entirely unconscious, but it is nonetheless a consequence of what we do. Maybe your book or something will help us to recognize that, and to figure out a way to be more open. But it happens everywhere, David, it happens in terms of the communities in which we live, the jobs that we hold, the people who are our family and friends. We like to be around people who think the way we do.

Jacobs: Do you notice how frequently the faculty and staff have lunch together?

Getz: I invited two staff people to our open house. They were shocked and declined very, very quickly. My sense was they were uncomfortable because they feel they didn't belong around the faculty. We do a whole lot more with students than we do with staff because they are of a different type. They're a "they. . . ."

My belief is that differences are an inevitable result of capitalism. That there will always be people who have more than others, and that there will always be people who have a lot more than some other people. That there will be great disparities. But I also think that if we get it to work, and that is a capital IF, but if we can get it to work, that capitalism and the free enterprise market system can produce a better life for the people at the bottom end of the scale. Even though they may look out there and see people who are a thousand times better off than they are, they will still be better off than they would have been if they were at the bottom end of the scale thirty years ago. So that over time—this is the rising tide argument, basically—that while they may be in a little raft instead of in a big ol' fancy yacht, their little raft will be higher than it once was. Now, there are a couple kinds of poverty. There is absolute poverty and there is relative poverty, and I don't think that relative poverty will ever go away. I don't think that absolute poverty is ever going to go away, but I think we will have a different point of view on it. I think that what constitutes absolute poverty in the minds of people will be different. I get the view of students from developing countries: they look around D.C. compared to the poverty in their home countries and they say, you think this is poor? And I think it is horrible what we have in D.C., but their perspective is, well, there are a lot of people in my country that would like to live like that. So the capitalistic system can improve the lot of all the social classes.... We will not ever be [the same] or have all the same material stuff.

NOTE

1. Interview with Professor Kathleen Getz, Washington, D.C., September 15, 1997.

REFERENCES

George, S. (1997). "How to win the war of ideas: Lessons from the Gramscian Right." *Dissent:* 47–53.

Hirshman, A. O. (1970). *Exit, voice, and loyalty: Responses to decline in organizations, firms, and states.* Cambridge, Mass.: Harvard University Press.

Monroe, K. R. (1995). *The heart of altruism: Perceptions of a common humanity.* Princeton, N.J.: Princeton University Press.

Niebuhr, R. (1944). *The children of light and the children of darkness: A vindication of democracy and a critique of its traditional defense.* New York: Charles Scribner's Sons.

A Liberal View

I interviewed Leon Shull, a leader of the liberal organization Americans for Democratic Action (ADA) since its
founding in 1947.[1] ADA has long served as a leader of
stakeholder coalitions, building alliances of civil rights
groups, organized labor, environmentalists, feminists, and
others. ADA had a Business Advisory Committee in its
first decades. Shull and I discussed the politics of business
and my hypothesis concerning the role of business lobbies
in foreclosing the possibility of compromise with stakeholders. I asked him if he recalled any significant business
involvement on behalf of the Civil Rights Act of 1964.

Leon Shull: Not significant, no, I can't hardly think of any involvement by business that was really helpful in the early days,
1964 or even since. . . . I don't recall or remember any. . . . I think
there were businessmen who were from time to time involved
with liberal organizations who were quite sympathetic to what
was going on. I can think of a few who were with ADA, people like
Marvin Rosenberg. He was a genuine liberal, no question about
that in my mind. . . .

He made curtains. I think he was the curtain king of the United States. . . .

Yes, I think it was a fairly substantial business, not the size of General Motors. . . . He was in every possible level that I could think . . . he was very liberal. . . .

I asked Shull whether he agreed with Edward Filene that liberal dissenters within the business community met considerable resistance from their colleagues.

Shull: . . . [T]here are very few business people who were active that way. I think there were people of wealth who were active [as liberal dissenters], and who [as a] matter of fact inherited their money and lived well off of it . . . and in terms of their times took advanced positions on things in what I would consider the right direction. I don't think their businesses did. I think the American owning classes have been a very hardened, tough class at all levels. . . .

I think what happened in Clinton's ill-fated effort to get . . . national health insurance [is that reformers were silenced by the rest of the business community]. That is where this certainly took place.

It took place at several levels where the Chamber of Commerce, which by announcement was quite prepared to support [national health insurance] in various ways, accepted the thesis that it could be done as sort . . . of government-employer supported program but under the impact of the opposition, was beaten into silence. And even the fellow who was the operating CEO (Richard Lesher) there really got beaten into silence, and I think that he has just recently retired. . . .

I think he just recently retired. And my impression is that he no longer had any influence after that happened. That he was really pushed aside because he'd gone that way, but he could hardly be called liberal, actually. . . .

I had several sessions with him, you know, over the years . . . he was rather a pleasant guy but rather conservative. [He took] a position which makes common sense. . . . People in the [Clinton] administration told me they were dreadfully disappointed by what the large corporations did. They were certain that this plan was so favorable to large corporations that they should be the most anxious to have it. I believe they thought they had a commitment. And people just walked away after the Chamber of Commerce thing happened and after the National Federation of Independent Businesses took up the cudgels. . . .

I hesitate to name because I'm not sure, but I would just say, my memory would say, the automobile companies, for example, complained bitterly about the heavy load. . . .

Yes, they went quiet. They were complaining bitterly about the heavy burden of health insurance . . . they were right, of course. Everybody went quiet. So, there was a power of the conservative movement to force people into line. Or at least they weren't willing to take up the fight. . . .

I asked Shull if he believed that the Olin Foundation and allied foundations played a significant role in reinforcing the extreme conservatism of the business lobbies and in supporting the "Southernization" of politics.

Shull: . . . I've read on some of that and I sort of believe it, but I don't know it. Yeah, I think [William Simon of the Olin Foundation has] played a role. I think, yeah, it seems to me I've seen his footprints everywhere. His name turns up, he's always sort of important [to projects of] the business community. I've never thought of, the way you put it, that he was trying to Southernize. . . . Why shouldn't they like the South? It's difficult to, you know . . . build unions down there. . . . Not a very friendly climate for unions, a very friendly climate for business. . . .

It didn't have to be. I guess it didn't have to be a conspiracy, in the sense that there [was] some Executive Council sitting down and planning at all. So, I think it's entirely possible in some ways these things happened even informally, don't you? People can be gathered in common interest talk. Obviously, there must have been moving spirits, for example, that put together things like the Heritage Foundation and groups like that. Look how fast they came up and how big they are. They're really a big outfit. [Liberals have] nothing that compares to them . . . the Brookings Institute doesn't . . . we are just lucky there are [a] few foundations around like 20th Century Fund [founded by Edward Filene] that still turn out some rather good stuff and keep working at it, but none of them have the same influence the Heritage, it seems to me, does. How do you explain, actually politically, the kind of failure of a liberal leadership to be aggressive and bold . . .

Shull argued that the litmus test for a progressive business organization like BSR should be its approach to collective bargaining.

Shull: See . . . I think that's the wedge issue, you know . . . that's the wedge issue it seems to me. . . . I've come to believe that more and more . . . because in the end you say: "Why the hell shouldn't these people be for civil rights?" Is there any evidence it has ever hurt them? What damage has it done? Why shouldn't they be for civil rights, if it's the right thing to be? And most people argue you shouldn't be discriminated against. . . .

Shull speculated about why businesses would oppose such a moderate measure as the Family Medical Leave Act.

Shull: . . . [B]ut it's the camel's nose [under the tent]. . . . I have [a parallel] fear [in the] opposite direction. You know that's how I react to the [conservative proposals on] entitlement programs. . . . [For example, the Republican initiative] permitting 390,000 seniors [to] buy into a special program [outside of Medicare]. What the hell does 390,000 mean? It doesn't mean a thing . . . except that I'm fearful. . . . Next time there'll be two million and then it'll be ten million or how many slots they need to [help] the healthy, wealthy people get out. . . . Yeah, in this bill it says they got full right to come back [into Medicare]. So, leave when you're healthy and come back when you're sick. I mean . . . talk about having a setup. If you're rich, you can't lose. . . .

NOTE

1. Interview with Leon Shull, Washington, D.C., August 25, 1997.

_____

CHAPTER FOURTEEN

Prospects for Progressive Business Politics

I have argued in the previous chapters that most associations of business subscribe to a philosophy that rejects compromise with stakeholders, particularly organized labor, in the formulation of private practice or public policy. Dissenting voices in the business community challenging the hard-line approach of the business associations are weak and seldom effective. The Republican party frequently intervenes in the affairs of business confederations to strengthen their resolve against compromise. In doing so, they are doing the will of many leading corporations.

My analysis is partly confirmed by commentary from the conservative journal, *The American Spectator*. Daniel Wattenberg warned in the June 1993 issue that the Chamber of Commerce was abandoning "bedrock free market principles" in efforts to build close relations with the Clinton administration (Wattenberg 1993). This article was itself a measure to assert conservative Republican hegemony over the Chamber. Senator Phil Gramm charged that Clinton was pursuing a strategy of "seduction and intimidation" to win support from segments of the business community for his program, thereby threatening the Republican coalition. Wattenberg blamed William Archey, the Chamber's Senior Vice President for Policy, for many of the Chamber's "liberal" aberrations, calling him a "liberal Trojan horse." (Archey had fired chief economist and consistent free market conservative Lawrence Hunter and, according to Wattenberg, led the Chamber to moderate its opposition to the Clinton economic plan, new taxes, and health care mandates.)

Republican conservatives grew increasingly dissatisfied with the Chamber's direction. On March 25, the House Republican leadership sent a letter to Chamber president Richard Lesher, criticizing the organization for an insufficiently aggressive response toward Clinton initiatives. The Republicans warned, "Your current posture is unacceptable. ... the ramifications could be quite severe. ... This has become a Republican Leadership issue. We intend to pursue our plans to make the Chamber a more effective advocate for free-market, pro-growth economic policies."

Chamber leader Ivan Gorr wrote in response, "This apparent attempt to dictate to us what our policies should be is deeply offensive. The irony of your approach will not be lost on our members—that a small group of legislators, who espouse the principle of limiting government interference in business, is attempting to interfere in the democratic policy-making process of a business organization." Wattenberg dismissed this analysis of Republican pressure on the Chamber. He argued instead that the Washington staff of the Chamber had departed from member views and that Republican leaders were merely asserting the will of the grassroots.

Wattenberg's essay in *The American Spectator* and this book provide coinciding analyses of the business lobbies despite conflicting normative assumptions. Wattenberg finds the prospect of business compromise with the welfare state to be treason to fundamental market principles. On the other hand, I find the lobbies' resistance to compromise to be a form of authoritarianism that obstructs justice and social progress. We agree on the contours of the divisions within the business community.

How likely is it that "moderate" and "progressive" employers (whom Wattenberg would regard as unprincipled pragmatists) might form an alternative "Chamber of Commerce" to contest the leadership of the mainstream business lobbies? Business for Social Responsibility (BSR) was, of course, organized partly in order to counter the Chamber on environmental and other regulatory issues. Unfortunately, member businesses found it difficult to agree on public policy recommendations, and BSR chose to refrain from lobbying. Moreover, few business leaders appear willing to endure criticism from their peers in mainstream business lobbies and the Republican party.

The National Planning Association (NPA), now the National Policy Association, is one of the few organizations in which labor and management leaders share deliberative councils. The affiliated committees of the NPA develop public and private policy recommendations, and labor and management seek consensus.

While the NPA has published many substantive reports demonstrating the potential of labor-management dialog, evidence of the limitations of this process is also striking. For example, there is a difference in the approach of unionists and employers. Labor leaders who participate continue to serve in a representative capacity. They are hopeful that they might win the enactment of many NPA recommendations in Congress. On the other hand, management participants tend to speak for themselves, not for large numbers of employers, and not even for their own firms. They are not likely to campaign for the adoption of their committee's recommendations. Employers view their

NPA work as a variant of philanthropy. It enhances their public stature but does not require that their everyday practices be altered. The NPA does not now appear to play as powerful a role in guiding employer behavior as does an organization like the Labor Policy Association (LPA).

The Committee for Economic Development (CED) is another business organization with a reputation for moderation and willingness to consider the views of other stakeholders. CED studies usually involve distinguished panels of experts from academia as well as business. As I have already noted, the CED has responded to pressure from business members to rescind their relatively advanced positions on social responsibility and related issues. While individual business executives with moderate views and some foundations no longer under the control of their business founders (e.g., the Ford Foundation) might promote CED initiatives that are stakeholder-sensitive, most power in the final analysis rests with conservative business.

The American Small Business Association (ASBA) is a new organization of dissident businesses committed to environmental protection, an adequate minimum wage, and an activist government. ASBA literature describes its mission as follows: "Through education, advocacy and lobbying, the ASBA speaks for small business people who believe that investing in our workers and communities is the best way to invest in our businesses" (ASBA 1996). It remains to be seen whether or not the ASBA will emerge as a significant progressive alternative to mainstream business lobbies or whether it will succumb to internal conflict or external pressure.

It might be possible to organize an enduring alliance of professionals and mid-level managers who could reasonably argue that they represent the progressive voice of business. This group might resemble to some degree the Independent Citizens Committee of the Arts, Sciences, and

Professions that the CIO sponsored in the mid-forties. The National Farmers Union, the Business and Professional Women, the National Medical Association (the African-American alternative to the AMA), and Vermont Business for Social Responsibility (which is much more ideologically cohesive than the national BSR and currently supports the ASBA) might be willing to join such an effort. Likely candidates for participation would be minority or feminist organizations in the business community who have the will to resist the influence of the LPA and its allies. The Farmers Union has long been associated with organized labor and can credibly argue that it represents small business. All of these groups have anchors that minimize their susceptibility to the pressure of chiselling business. When the LPA, the Chamber, and the NAM initiate an offensive on a public policy question, the progressive business/professional alliance that I have described might effectively respond, explaining why the LPA's vision of competitiveness and flexibility would be disastrous for the majority of Americans.

The philosophy that would animate this progressive business organization would be one of *praxis* rather than traditional management. That is, "action," which Aristotle distinguished from labor and work and Hannah Arendt reconceived for the modern era (Arendt 1958).

Aristotle defined labor as the set of activities necessary for the subsistence of the household. Labor resulted in things immediately consumed by the household and was performed by slaves in the Greek city-state. Work, on the other hand, creates an enduring product which proves the mastery of the worker over matter to the public at large. Action is the process of creation, innovation, and self-expression that characterizes the life of the citizen. It is civic action.

Hannah Arendt linked action and the plurality of autonomous voices that describe the human condition:

Human plurality, the basic condition of both action and speech, has the twofold character of equality and distinction. If men were not equal, they could neither understand each other and those who became before them nor plan for the future and foresee the needs of those who will come after them. If men were not distinct, each human being distinguished from any other who was, or will ever be, they would need neither speech nor action to make themselves understood. Signs and sounds to communicate immediate, identical needs and wants would be enough. (1958, pp. 175–176)

Managing is a form of action which tends to generate privilege as a product. It limits the benefits of action to the leaders of the organization. A business association fully open to dialog with stakeholders would embrace action in the broader sense. (It would also be structured in such a way as to stimulate dialog. That is, less powerful stakeholders—minority managers, labor, and other constituencies—would be represented.)

REFERENCES

Arendt, H. (1958). *The human condition*. Chicago: University of Chicago Press.

ASBA. (1996). http://www.legendinc.com/FolderLinc/ASBAHQ/Pages/VotersGuide.

Wattenberg, D. (1993). "Clinton's echo chamber." *The American Spectator* (June): 18–23.

Is Business a "System of Power"?

On April 8, 1998, Jerry Jasinowski addressed the Board of Directors of the National Association of Manufacturers (NAM) and provided his view of the opportunities facing the NAM. His speech illuminates the philosophy of NAM. The rigid conservatism described by Alfred Cleveland (1848) in his *Harvard Business Review* article is still evident. Jasinowski embraces several important principles:

First, the NAM works to maximize solidarity among organizations representing the business community. NAM lobbying is guided by the assumption that there should be a unified business position. Jasinowski argues that his association is "industry's chief consensus-builder."

Second, the NAM seeks to emphasize the role of small manufacturers in its councils to improve its image. Jasinowski states, "To strengthen the voice of our small members, building on the leadership of this board, we are creating a President's Council of influential small manufacturers all across the country. Small manufacturers are often the best advocates for manufacturing." This approach is unlikely to generate a debate within the NAM as to the coincidence or divergence of interests among small and large enterprises. Jasinowski proposes, in effect, that the NAM leadership develop the vanguard for small business.

Third, the NAM claims to represent employees as well as employers. The NAM has endorsed the TEAM Act and supports "employee involvement." That is, the NAM favors employee involvement in enterprise decision-making as long as employers choose those who speak for employees. Moreover, the Association seeks to mobilize employees in the pursuit of its agenda through, for example, the ELAN program at Eastman Chemical, which "helps workers gain access to the political process, often on issues that are in our common interest." NAM supports so-called "paycheck protection" legislation, which would mandate employee votes on all union political expenditures. In other words, the NAM's concept of legitimate employee involvement in the enterprise and in the political process is contingent upon employer agreement.

The NAM claims membership in the "power elite" in an ironic turn of phrase (See Mills [1956]).

REMARKS PREPARED FOR DELIVERY TO THE NAM BOARD OF DIRECTORS BY JERRY J. JASINOWSKI, PRESIDENT AND CEO, NATIONAL ASSOCIATION OF MANUFACTURERS, APRIL 3, 1998

It's wonderful to be back with the NAM's board and to give you a positive report on the state of your organization. Thanks in large part to the contributions each of you is making, our economy is strong and the quality of American life is improving. More people are working than at any time in our history. Compensation is up and going higher. Inflation is almost an afterthought.

Interest rates are stable and consumers are confident. And manufacturing has become a productivity powerhouse.

These things don't just happen. They happen because men and women like you are working for standards of excellence in your companies, in your associations and in our country. . . .

But I want to go beyond the report and make ten points about who we are and what we're doing. All of these points are heavily dependent on your contributions and the team culture that is part of the NAM.

First, the NAM is a recognized part of Washington's power elite. In December, *Fortune* magazine published a major survey of 2,200 of Washington's insiders—members of Congress, their staffs and the administration. The survey asked a simple question—what organizations are the most powerful in Washington?

One hundred and twenty-five organizations were mentioned. And when *Fortune* listed what it called "The Power 25," the NAM was number thirteen—the highest rating of any broad-based business group. Our quotes and comments and columns about interest rates, the Asian financial crisis, global climate change, our impending skills shortage, productivity and technology and health care reform have been used in major newspapers and on such television programs as *NBC Nightly News, Nightline,* the *Nightly Business Report,* CNBC's *Market Wrap,* CNN, *CBS News* and National Public Radio.

We're making our presence felt in the media and on Capitol Hill. And that's why our agenda is now influencing Washington's agenda—and why this influence will continue in the future. . . .

And remember: although our 14,000 companies represent 85 percent of the manufacturing output in the U.S., we're aware that we're not the only game in town. We make it a point to help mobilize other important business groups, particularly the Business Roundtable, the U.S. Chamber of Commerce and major trade organizations. I see it as part of my job to pull all the business groups together.

It's because of the NAM's unusual credibility and aggressive approach to making our case in the halls of government that my third point, on our recent legislative and policy successes, is an easy story for me to tell. Here are some of the things the NAM has been advancing, successfully, in Congress and the Administration:

The Senate has passed legislation authorizing funding for the International Monetary Fund to help address the Asian financial turmoil. The highway bill, whose acronym is "ISTEA," will fund freeways, bridges and many transportation improvements so our transportation-intensive economy can move ahead. We're helping to move forward an immigration reform bill that will let more high-technology workers come into our country from abroad and we have made progress on legislation that would consolidate all federal training programs. We're making an aggressive case for the R&D tax credit, patent reform and are working hard to find a suitable compromise on encryption policy.

We're gaining ground on reforming Social Security. Everyone from conservatives like Newt Gingrich to liberals like Daniel Patrick Moynihan are calling for private investment accounts that would let Americans build real wealth for their retirements. I especially want to recognize our former chairman, Warren Batts, for his leadership on this issue.

Securities litigation reform is building steam in the Senate. This effort is important to many of you as you try to build strong companies without the threat of lawsuits by predatory attorneys. The bipartisan regulatory reform bill authored by Senators Thompson and Levin is also a priority for us and we are working with the Senators to gain additional bipartisan sponsors, particularly on the Democratic side of the aisle.

And just a few weeks ago, the Senate passed an amendment to the highway bill authored by Senator Jim Inhofe of Oklahoma that would require the scientifically-sound application of clean air standards approved last year by the President. If signed into law, this proposal will stop some of the worst excesses of the EPA's clean air mandates.

And we're working hard and successfully to prevent bad bills on health care, the global climate debate and many other areas from becoming law. . . .

As you can see, we're moving ahead on a variety of fronts. But let me qualify what I've just said in one important way: The achievements of the 105th Congress and the Clinton White

House have been modest, at best. This fact underscores the fourth point I want to emphasize. There has seldom been a time when business leadership has been more needed in Washington—and the NAM is there to help lead the way. . . .

[T]he GOP seems ambivalent about the business agenda. Some Republicans are pro-business, pro-trade, pro-growth. Others are wary of international trade and other important growth policies. There is a clear need to help them understand the political power of our pro-growth agenda. . . .

The good news is that business can fill this rather large vacuum. According to a poll conducted by Rasmussen Research in January, here's how the American people respond when asked who deserves credit for the economy: 22 percent say the President, 14 percent tip their hats to the Congress. But 51 percent acknowledge that business is the main reason why the economy is booming.

That's a pretty encouraging statistic. It shows that the public is beginning to recognize that business and manufacturing are the role models for success, and that we know how to make the right decisions about increasing the growth of our economy.

Manufacturing is making long-term contributions to our country. That's the fifth point I want to discuss with you.

The Manufacturing Institute is the educational arm of the NAM and is chaired by John Correnti of Nucor Steel. The Institute is getting the facts out about manufacturing's contributions to the economy: through studies, a series on manufacturing success stories, press events, National Manufacturing Week and other means.

We're also holding a major Earth Day event later this month on the Ellipse outside the White House. This event is part of our series of events highlighting manufacturing success stories. Companies from around the country will be displaying their latest environmentally friendly products and will show that the manufacturers of America are our country's leading environmentalists. There are still some slots open for those of you who would like to participate in this event.

And the NAM's new Center for Workforce Success, a division of the Manufacturing Institute, is making the case for excellence among our workers. We're committed to ensuring that industry has the quality and quantity of workers needed to do the high-tech jobs demanded by the new global economy.

In partnership with Arthur Anderson, we've also established NAM Awards for Workforce Excellence, which give $10,000 prizes to worker teams. We are creating a special cadre of manufacturing executives who will be spokespeople for education and training in the workforce.

It is because the worker is central to the success of our economy that my sixth point is so important: Manufacturing—and the NAM—were right about our capacity to grow without inflation accelerating. But growth is contingent on our employees, which is why our new emphasis is on the American worker.

As my new book emphasizes, we can have a Rising Tide if we follow the right policies. One of the NAM's greatest successes in the past eighteen months has been to help dissuade the Federal Reserve Board from raising interest rates. Raising rates would cripple growth. And we've made our case effectively and persuasively.

But as we continue to fight rate hikes and argue for growth, we also have to remember that growth will not continue unless we address the needs of the millions of men and women who are making things in America.

Technology, training, trade and taxes—these are the "four t's" that will help our workers retain their strong foothold in the world economy. Let me discuss each of them briefly because they are central to advocating a positive agenda.

Although current estimations are inexact, it's reasonable to say that about two-thirds of productivity growth in the 1990s and about one-third of all growth in non-farm business is due to technology. Workers with high-tech jobs earn more and have greater professional challenges than many other workers. Staying on the leading edge of technology is one of the greatest issues confronting industry today. That's where training comes in.

We need a workforce that can perform increasingly complex tasks. Yet as many of you know, it's getting harder to find qualified employees. Training employees through improvements in our educational system and through employer efforts is critical to our economic success.

So is increased trade. Trade means higher compensation, higher benefits and more secure jobs for our workers. We need to advance pro-trade policies both for the overall growth of the economy and, contrary to what the protectionists say, for the sake of secure, well-paying jobs for our employees.

And last but not least, the "fourth t": tax reform. Lower, fairer taxes on individuals and businesses is important to improve the quality of workers' lives and to the growth of our economy.

In the past few moments I've recounted a number of our priorities and successes. But these successes . . . didn't just happen. The reason we've been so active and effective is what I want to talk about in my seventh point. The NAM is where we are today because we are able to marshal the power of an unusually broad-based business association and our capacity to work at the grass roots all around the country.

The NAM is the coalition leader of many industry and business organizations throughout Washington. We are active in working with state associations, learning about their members' needs and helping them advance manufacturing's agenda in Washington. We work with all the narrower industry groups on issues of common concern, adding a great deal of clout to the policy projects that are important to all of industry. As the *Fortune* survey I mentioned earlier suggests, we are bringing clout to industry's fights.

We are industry's chief consensus builder. Right now, I'm pushing the Business Roundtable and the Chamber of Commerce to join us in a coordinated effort to prevent union partisanship from being successful. This includes working together to back paycheck protection proposals across America. Unions have no right to just take their members' money and use it for partisan purposes without their members' consent.

That's just one example of the NAM's consistent, effective leadership in the business community. We are the umbrella group that draws together the sometimes-disparate chords of large, small and mid-sized business groups and keeps all of us on the same page. We look for common ground and use it to fight industry's battles.

Clearly, one of the keys to fighting those battles is strengthening our small and mid-sized manufacturers. Our efforts to that end constitute my eighth point. To strengthen the voice of our small members, building on the leadership of this board, we are creating a President's Council of influential small manufacturers all across the country. Small manufacturers are often the best advocates for manufacturing.

One of the heaviest burdens born by the NAM's 10,000 members that are small and medium manufacturers is the estate, or "death," tax. We've launched a full-scale effort to kill the death tax before it kills any additional small and family-owned businesses.

But all the lobbying efforts and legislative successes and member services in the world are no substitute for your own work to move the political system in your communities and states and here in Washington. My ninth point is exactly that—member involvement is key to the NAM's continued success.

To paraphrase Alexis de Tocqueville, "An American manufacturing association is a powerful and enlightened member of the community which, by defending its own rights, saves the common liberties of the country."

We have the freedom in our country to shape its future. And it's time to use what de Tocqueville called "our common liberties" to end the domination by politicians about the common interests of America.

NAM members manufacture their wares in virtually every congressional district in the nation. We are a key constituency of every man and woman serving on Capitol Hill. How do we get their attention? Simple: In the words of Washington lobbyist Tom Boggs, himself the son of a congressman, "The best way to communicate with Congress is through a Congressman."

We urge you to contact your Representatives and Senators personally. Meet with them when they're back home and conduct plant tours. Call them on the phone and give your advice on issues. Work with local member groups and join in local NAM meetings with the people who represent you in the House and Senate.

But your work is not enough. That's my tenth point: employee involvement is crucial for the success of our agenda. Our Chairman, Earnie Deavenport, has initiated an extensive employee involvement network at Eastman Chemical. It's called the "ELAN" program, and helps workers gain access to the political process, often on issues that are in our common interest.

Similarly, Bill Hudson, next year's Chairman and a leader on international trade, also knows the power of employee persuasion. He's working to help the 7,500 AMP employees in Congressman George Gekas' district in Pennsylvania make their voices heard loud and clear. Your commitment, and that of your employees, to making our case at the local and regional level reinforces the NAM's efforts in Washington. And that helps us not only make our case, but also lead and shape public opinion. When the eighteen million men and women who make things in America speak up, politicians will listen—and will act. . . .

Ultimately, we're about four things:

- A clear voice with a pro-growth, pro-manufacturing, pro-worker message.

- A broad and increasingly active membership of employers and employees who engage in real grassroots activity.

- Coalition building and leadership that enables the business community to be united and speak with one voice.

- And unrivaled media credibility and visibility.

REFERENCES

Cleveland, A. (1948). "NAM: Spokesman for industry?" *Harvard Business Review* (May 26).

Mills, C. W. (1956). *The power elite*. New York: Oxford University Press.

BSR Board of Directors

The membership of the Board of Directors of Business for Social Responsibility is a diverse group, including both founding members with ties to the more ideologically cohesive Social Venture Network and more recently admitted business leaders with more mainstream politics and credentials. Given this diversity, it is difficulty for the Board to reach consensus on public policy issues.

CO-CHAIRS (BSR 1997)

ARNOLD HIATT is Chairman of The Stride Rite Foundation. Prior to this position, he served as Chairman, CEO and President of The Stride Rite Corporation. Under Mr. Hiatt's leadership, the Stride Rite Corporation received numerous recognitions for its work in corporate citizenship, including Columbia University's Lawrence A. Wien Prize in Corporate Social Responsibility in 1992 and Harvard University's George S. Dively Award for Corporate Public Initiative in 1991. Mr. Hiatt is on the Board of Directors for The Cabot Corporation and Dreyfus Corporation and is a trustee of the Isabella Stewart Gardner Museum, the John Merck Fund and Northeastern University.

HELEN MILLS is Senior Vice President of Aon Consulting, with responsibilities for the following areas: domestic and international benefits issues, benefit planning and competitive positioning in the marketplace. In addition to her responsibilities with Aon Consulting, Ms. Mills serves as President of the Soapbox Trading Company, the first American franchise of the U.K. based retailer, The Body Shop. She also serves as Vice President of City Works, a company which creates jobs in the inner city of Washington, D.C., by screen-printing T-shirts. Ms. Mills was awarded the 1992 Entrepreneur of the Year Award in the women-owned business category and is a recipient of the 1996 District of Columbia Chamber of Commerce Rudd-Turner Awards for Inspirational Leadership. She is on the Board of Directors of the Social Venture Network and is a member of the Business Leadership Council of the Points of Light Foundation.

PRESIDENT

BOB DUNN has been President and CEO of BSR and the BSR Education Fund since December 1994, and has served on the Board of Directors since 1993. For the prior thirteen years, Mr. Dunn worked at Levi Strauss & Company, where he was Vice President of Corporate Affairs and Executive Vice President of the Levi Strauss Foundation, overseeing the company's corporate communications, community affairs, and government affairs. He also counseled senior management on issues of corporate social responsibility. Mr. Dunn previously served as Deputy Appointments Secretary to former President Jimmy Carter, Executive Assistant to the U.S. Ambassador to Mexico, Secretary of the

Department of Administration, and Chief of Staff to the Governor of the State of Wisconsin. Mr. Dunn also serves as a member of the Board of the Yerba Buena Center for the Arts and the Jacobson Foundation, chairs the screening committee for the Koret Israel Prize, and serves on the awards screening committee for the Points of Light Foundation and the National Advisory Committee for Students for Responsible Business.

BOARD OF DIRECTORS

RAY ANDERSON is Founder, Chairman, President, and CEO of Interface, Inc., one of the world's largest interior furnishings companies. Mr. Anderson was awarded the 1992 International Businessman of the Year Award by the Society of International Business Fellows, the 1996 Ernst & Young Entrepreneur of the Year Award for the Southeast Region, and the 1996 Global Green USA Millennium Award for Corporate Environmental Leadership. Mr. Anderson is on the Board of Directors for Bank South Corporation, NationsBank Corporation, and Royal Ten Cate. He is also Chairman of the Georgia Tech Advisory Board, Member of the President's Council for Sustainable Development, and Member of the Advisory Board for the School of Architecture at the University of Virginia.

JOAN BOK is Chairman of New England Electric System (NEES), a public utility holding company. NEES provides electric service to over 3 million people in Massachusetts, Rhode Island, and New Hampshire through its retail subsidiaries—Massachusetts Electric Company, The Narragansett Electric Company, and Granite State Electric Company. In addition to her job as chairman, Ms. Bok chairs the board's executive committee and serves as a director for most NEES companies' boards. She serves on the Board of Directors for Avery Dennison Corporation, John

Hancock Mutual Life Insurance Company and Monsanto Company. She is also on the Board of Trustees of the Boston Athenaeum, The Urban Institute, Woods Hole Oceanographic Institution and the Worcester Foundation for Biomedical Research. Ms. Bok is a former President of the Harvard Board of Overseers.

CHRISTIE BOULDING is Treasurer and CFO of Graham Contracting Inc., a design and construction firm specializing in residential and commercial renovations in the Boston area. Prior to Graham Contracting, Ms. Boulding was the Assistant Vice President of the Bank of Boston's High Technology Division, where she developed and implemented a loan review system within the division. Ms. Boulding is on the Steering Committee for BSR Greater Boston.

DONNA CALLEJON is Senior Vice President for Corporate Development of Fannie Mae. She is responsible for leading the company's efforts in strategic planning, industry analysis, and economics. Ms. Callejon joined Fannie Mae in 1986 and has held a number of positions in the areas of risk management, negotiated transactions, and product acquisition. In 1991, she was named Senior Vice President for Single-Family Business, a position she held until July 1996. Prior to joining Fannie Mae, Ms. Callejon held several positions in sales and trading at Farmers Savings Bank in California.

SHARON COHEN is Vice President of Public Affairs at Reebok and Executive Director of The Reebok Foundation. Prior to this, Ms. Cohen was Vice President of Advertising. Ms. Cohen was instrumental in developing the Reebok Human Rights Award, which celebrates the achievements of young human rights activists. Ms. Cohen is on the Board of

Directors for Social Venture Network and The Boston Coalition.

GUN DENHART is the Co-Founder and Chairman of Hanna Andersson, a children's clothing catalog that was started in 1983. The company is widely known for its Hannadowns program, which encourages customers to send back their used Hanna Andersson clothing for a 20 percent credit of the original purchase price. The company then donates 5 percent of profits to charities that benefit women and children. She is a founding member of BSR and is a member of the Board of Directors of Bright Horizons Children's Centers, Camera World, and Children First for Oregon. Ms. Denhart received the 1992 Business Enterprise Award and has been recognized by *Working Woman* magazine in their annual "100 Best Companies for Working Mothers" for support of working women and their families for the past five years.

RON GRZYWINSKI is Chairman and CEO of Shorebank Corporation, a commercial bank holding company that finances and implements for-profit and not-for-profit community development strategies. In addition to his chairmanship at Shorebank Corporation, Mr. Grzywinski does short-term consulting for international donors who have capitalized micro-enterprise loan programs in Bangladesh and Pakistan. Mr. Grzywinski is also on the Board of Directors or Trustees of the Center for Community Change, Corporation for Enterprise Development, Development Training Institute, Enterprise Development Company, The Enterprise Foundation, and Private Agencies Collaborating Together.

ALAN HASSENFELD is Chairman and CEO of Hasbro, Inc., a worldwide leader in the design, manufacture, and marketing of toys, games, puzzles, and infant care products. Prior to his current position, Mr. Hassenfeld served as President, Executive Vice President, Vice President of Marketing and Sales, Vice President of International Operations, and Assistant to the President. Mr. Hassenfeld has received various awards, including the 1993 Humanitarian Award by the Institute for International Sport, the 1993 Excellence in Family Business Management Award by Bryant College Institute for Family Enterprise, and the 1993 Community Service Award by the Rhode Island Section of the National Council of Jewish Women. He is on the Board of Directors for the Association of Governing Boards of Universities and Colleges, Hasbro Children's Foundation, Hasbro, Inc., Jewish Federation of Rhode Island, The Jewish Foundation, and Refugees International.

ELLIOT HOFFMAN is the President of Just Desserts, a retail and wholesale bakery located in the San Francisco Bay Area. Mr. Hoffman and the company have received numerous awards for their socially responsible practices, including one of California's Ten Best Employers by *California* magazine, the U.S. Small Business Administration's Small Business Growth Award, the Chamber of Commerce's Excellence in Business Award, and one of ten outstanding entrepreneurs in San Francisco. Mr. Hoffman is involved in a number of civic efforts, including San Franciscans for Sensible Government, the San Francisco Chamber of Commerce, and San Francisco 2000. He co-founded and serves on the board of The Garden Project.

BRUCE KLATSKY is Chairman, President, and Chief Executive Officer of Phillips-Van Heusen Corporation, one of the world's largest apparel and footwear companies. In 1995, Mr. Klatsky also led the company's acquisition of the apparel division of Crystal Brands, Inc., adding Izod and Gant to Phillips-Van Heusen's roster of leading national brands, which includes Van Heusen dress shirts, Geoffrey

Beene designer shirts, and G. H. Bass men's and women's casual shoes. Mr. Klatsky is a charter member of The Human Rights Watch Council, a trustee of Case Western Reserve University, and a member of the Board of Directors and the Executive Committee of the American Apparel Manufacturers Association. He served as an advisor on U.S. trade policy in the administrations of former Presidents Reagan and Bush.

DOMINIC KULIK is Co-founder and CEO of Take the Lead, Inc., a company that manufactures and markets organic and recycled cotton apparel and donates 10 percent of its profits to children's and environmental organizations. Mr. Kulik was also the co-founder and co-director of LEAD, USA, a national non-profit educational institute promoting creative solutions to global problems.

JOSH MAILMAN is the President of Sirius Business Corporation, an investment management corporation. He is a private investor in a number of businesses related to ecological sustainability in the United States and developing countries, including Sharman Pharmaceutical, Energia Global, Seeds of Change, and Green Technologies. Mr. Mailman is a founding investor in Utne Reader, Stonyfield Farms, Juniper Partners, and Calvert Social Venture Partners. He was a founding member of BSR and is a member of the Board of Directors of Human Rights Watch, International Rivers Network, and the Living Earth Foundation in the United Kingdom

JOHN ONODA is Vice President of Worldwide Communications at General Motors Corporation (GM). In this capacity, he oversees media relations, executive communications, employee communications, issues and crises management, financial communications, speech writing, video communications, and corporate Internet and intranet activities. He is also Chairman of GM's Communications Strategy Council. Prior to his current position, Mr. Onoda held various executive positions, including Vice President of Corporate Communications for Levi Strauss & Co., Director of Media Relations for McDonald's Corporation, Director of External Communications for Holiday Corporation, and Senior Communications Associate for Mitchell Energy & Development Corporation.

COLEMAN PETERSON is Senior Vice President of the People Division of Wal-Mart Stores, Inc. He is responsible for all Human Resources activities of the Corporation and sets companywide personnel direction and strategies for an employee base of over 500,000 associates internationally. Prior to this position, Mr. Peterson was Senior Vice President of Human Resources and Vice President of Organizational Development at Venture Stores, Inc. Mr. Peterson serves on the Advisory Boards for the University of Florida Retail Institute and the Florida A&M's President's Council. He has also served on the Board of Directors and Advisory Boards in St. Louis for The United Way, Urban League of Metropolitan, United Negro College Fund, and Junior League.

HARRY QUADRACCI is President and Founder of Quad/Graphics, Inc., a leading printing, technology, and media company, with over 900 magazine and catalog clients throughout the United States Mr. Quadracci has received numerous awards, including the Printing Industry Hall of Fame in 1986 by *Printing Impressions* magazine and the Rochester Institute of Technology; the Grow Wisconsin Business Award in 1984; and the Wisconsin Sales & Marketing Executive of the Year in 1986.

MITCHELL ROFSKY is the President of American Consumer Insurance, an insurance agency that provides automobile and homeowners insurance. The agency uses a model that provides 1 percent of its gross premium to nonprofits focused on the consumer/environmental impact of the automobile. The agency also provides safety information to its customers through a "Consumer Hot-line." Mr. Rofsky is the former President of Working Assets Capital Management and spent most of the 1980s as Executive Vice President of the National Cooperative Bank and President of the National Cooperative Bank Development Corporation. Mr. Rofsky is also the former Chair of the BSR Board.

ROGER SANT is Co-Founder and Chairman of the Board of The AES Corporation, one of the largest global power producers. Prior to founding AES, Mr. Sant was Director of the Mellon Institute's Energy Productivity Center. During this period he became widely known as the author of "The Least-Cost Energy Strategy"—in which the goal of providing energy services to the consumer at the least possible cost supersedes other energy objectives. He also served as a political appointee in the Ford Administration and taught corporate finance at the Stanford University Graduate School of Business. Mr. Sant is Chairman of the World Wildlife Fund and is on the Board of Directors and Trustees of Marriott International, Inc., The National Symphony Orchestra, the World Wide Fund for Nature, and the World Resources Institute. He is also a member of the Aspen Institute's Committee on Energy and the National Council of the Environmental Defense Fund.

LAURA SCHER is Chief Executive Officer and Co-founder of Working Assets Funding Services, a long distance and credit card company that makes donations to nonprofit organizations. Since 1985, the company has donated more than $7 million to nonprofits. Ms. Scher is a leading spokesperson for businesses that have social as well as financial objectives. She is on the Board of Directors for the Telecommunications Resellers Association and Community Products, Inc.

GAIL SNOWDEN is President of First Community Bank at BankBoston, a multi-state business unit that works to meet the basic banking and credit needs of inner-city residents and businesses throughout New England. Ms. Snowden is responsible for BankBoston's network of inner-city neighborhood branches and loan production resource centers, along with its community-based lending operation. She has received numerous awards, including the 1992 SBA Small Business Minority Business Advocate of the Year, the Boston Urban Bankers Forum Outstanding Member, the National Association of Urban Bankers Outstanding Member, the YMCA Black Achievers Award, the New England Women's Leadership Award in 1993, and was named one of the nation's Top Business and Professional Women by *Dollars and Sense* magazine in 1993. She is on the Board of Directors for Massachusetts Industrial Finance Agency and the American Student Assistance Corp., and has served as Advisory Committee Chairman and President of the National Association of Urban Bankers Forum.

DEBEN TOBIAS is Vice President of Finance and Administration and Chief Financial Officer of Bolder Heuristics, Inc., a software development company. Prior to this position, Mr. Tobias founded and managed two entrepreneurial efforts—Colony Finance Corporation in Boston, Massachusetts, and The Franklin School of Contemporary Studies in London, England. He also has managed Circle Health Center in Boulder, Colorado. He is Co-Chair of the BSR Colorado Network.

ELLA D. WILLIAMS is the President and CEO of Aegir Systems, an engineering and computer services firm. Ms. Williams is opening Ella's World Class Cheesecakes, Breads and Muffins, a bakery that will create more jobs for inner-city youth in Los Angeles and will educate 100 minority students with a portion of the proceeds. She has received national recognition for her accomplishments, including one of the Nation's Ten Most Admired Women Managers of 1993 by *Working Woman*, Entrepreneur of the Year by AT&T, and one of five entrepreneurs nationwide to receive the Woman of Enterprise award from the Small Business Administration and Avon Products.

REFERENCE

BSR. (1997). *Board of directors*. Http://www.bsr.org/bsrboard.htm.

Selected Bibliography

Arendt, H. (1958). *The human condition*. Chicago: University of Chicago Press.

Baumol, W., R. Likert, H. C. Wallich, and J. J. McGowan. (1970). *A new rationale for corporate social policy*. New York: Committee for Economic Development.

Boulware, L. R. (1969). *The truth about Boulwarism: Trying to do right voluntarily*. Washington, D.C.: Bureau of National Affairs.

Brady, R. (1943). *Business as a system of power*. New York: Columbia University Press.

Cleveland, A. (1948). "NAM: Spokesman for industry?" *Harvard Business Review* (May 26).

Cohen, J., and J. Rogers. (1992). "Secondary associations and democratic governance." *Politics and Society* 20: 393–472.

Committee for Economic Development. (1971). *Social responsibilities of business corporations*. New York: Committee for Economic Development.

Dewey, J. (1939). "Democracy and educational administration." In Ratner, J., ed., *Intelligence in the modern world*. New York: Random House, pp. 400–404.

Dunlop, J. (1984). *Dispute resolution: Negotiations and consensus building*. Dover, Mass.: Auburn House.

Filene, E. A. (1924). *The way out: A forecast of coming changes in American business and industry*. Garden City, N.Y.: Doubleday, Page & Company.

Frederick, W. C. (1981). "Free market vs. social responsibility." *California management review* 23: 20–28.

Gould, W. L. (1993). *Agenda for reform*. Cambridge, Mass.: M.I.T. Press.

Green, M. (1996). *Epitaph for American labor: How union leaders lost touch with America*. Washington, D.C.: AEI Press.

Gross, J. (1995). *Subverting the promise*. Philadelphia: Temple University Press.

Grunberger, F. V. (1980). *Prophets without honor*. New York: McGraw-Hill.

Hirshman, A. O. (1970). *Exit, voice, and loyalty: Responses to decline in organizations, firms, and states*. Cambridge, Mass.: Harvard University Press.

Hood, J. M. (1996). *The heroic enterprise: Business and the common good*. New York: The Free Press.

Jacoby, S., ed. (1991). *Masters to managers: Historical and comparative perspectives on American employers*. New York: Columbia University Press.

Levitan, S. A., and M. Cooper. (1984). *Business lobbies: The public good and the bottom line*. Baltimore: Johns Hopkins University Press.

Lind, M. (1996). *Up from conservatism: Why the right is wrong for America*. New York: The Free Press.

Lowi, T. J. (1969). *The end of liberalism*. New York: Norton.

Maraniss, D., and M. Weisskopf. (1996). *"Tell Newt to shut up."* New York: Touchstone.

Mill, J. S. (1974). *On liberty*. New York: Appleton-Century Crofts.

Mills, C. W. (1948). *The new men of power: America's labor leaders*. New York: Harcourt Brace.

Mills, C. W. (1956). *The power elite*. New York: Oxford University Press.

Monroe, K. R. (1995). *The heart of altruism: Perceptions of a common humanity.* Princeton, N.J.: Princeton University Press.

Niebuhr, R. (1944). *The children of light and the children of darkness.* New York: Scribner's.

Pinker, S. (1995). *The language instinct.* New York: HarperCollins.

Piore, M. (1995). *Beyond liberalism.* Cambridge, Mass.: Harvard University Press.

Post, J. E., W. C. Frederick, A. T. Lawrence, and J. Weber. (1996). *Business and society: Corporate strategy, public policy, ethics.* New York: McGraw-Hill.

Potter, E. E., and J. A. Youngman. (1995). *Keeping America competitive: Employment policy for the twenty-first century.* Lakewood, Colo.: Glenbridge Publishing.

Rosenblum, Jonathan D. (1995). *Copper crucible.* Ithaca, N.Y.: ILR Press.

Saloma, J. S., III. (1984). *Ominous politics: The new conservative labyrinth.* New York: Hill and Wang.

Thelen, D. (1976). *Robert M. La Follette and the insurgent spirit.* Boston: Little, Brown.

Viereck, P. (1949). *Conservatism revisited: The revolt against revolt: 1815–1949.* New York: Scribner's.

Index

About the Author

DAVID C. D. JACOBS is Associate Professor at the Kogod College of Business Administration, American University–Washington, D.C. He teaches courses on industrial relations and business and society, consults for trade unions, and serves on the national board of Americans for Democratic Action. He is the author of *Collective Bargaining as an Instrument of Social Change* (1994) and other writings in the journals of his fields.